DON'T BE AFRAID TO DISCIPLINE

DON'T BE AFRAID TO DISCIPLINE

Dr. Ruth Peters

Golden Books
New York

Golden Books®
888 Seventh Avenue
New York, NY 10106

Golden Books® and colophon
are trademarks of Golden Books Publishing Co., Inc.

Designed by Suzanne Noli

Manufactured in the United States of America

1 3 5 7 9 10 8 6 4 2

Library of Congress Cataloging-in-Publication Data
Peters, Ruth Allen.
Don't be afraid to discipline / Ruth Peters.
p. cm.
Includes bibliographical references and index.
ISBN 0-307-44001-X (alk. paper)
1. Discipline of children. 2. Child rearing.
3. Problem children—Behavior modification. 4. Parent and child.
5. Parent and teenager. 6. Parenting.   I. Title.
HQ770.4.P4664   1997
649'.64—dc21   97-15182
                                                      CIP

To my families—past and present—for honoring me
with their love

CONFIDENTIALITY NOTE

Names and identifying details in the case histories reported within this book have been changed. All reported cases are real, and permission to report them has been given by the parent or guardian.

ACKNOWLEDGMENTS

I would like to thank the many families who have worked with me for more than two decades, as we learned from each other what parenting is all about! Special thanks to the brave parents and kids who have shared their experiences with my readers in an effort to help others learn from them.

My heartfelt appreciation to my transcription staff, Harriet Coren and Jean Loveland, who were ready at the drop of a hat to work on revisions as the book took shape.

Ashley Carroll and Jan Miller, my literary agents, deserve sincere acknowledgment for their faith in my ideas and my belief that parents want to be the best that they can be.

A very special thank you to my editors at Golden Books: Laura Yorke for her exquisite insights and uncanny organizational ability, and Cassie Jones for her creative editing, supportive attitude, and most of all, her patience. Also, sincere appreciation to Bob Asahina for seeing the importance of this project and making it a reality.

And, finally, hugs and kisses to my husband and kids for their patience and support, both when I had writer's block and when I couldn't seem to stop writing!

CONTENTS

INTRODUCTION:

One Step Ahead of Our Kids

Who died and left you in charge?" is one of my husband's favorite comebacks when I have made a command decision about either of our two children. Sometimes I think that he was put here on earth to remind me that although I'm a longtime mom and a middle-aged psychologist, I don't know everything there is to know about child rearing. In fact, my children teach me something new almost every day!

So I begin this book with a disclaimer: I know a lot about kids and what makes them tick, but I also realize how challenging parenting can be. Having read a multitude of developmental psychology texts as well as most of the popular child-rearing books, I'm familiar with the current child-raising philosophies. But what has really helped to develop my parenting skills has been my eighteen years of mothering and over twenty years of helping hundreds of families raise their children. That's a lot of time spent dealing with kid issues and trying to figure out how to solve typical family problems.

Sometimes I think that I've heard it all and begin to become a bit cocky. But no sooner do I pronounce that a certain case is no big deal, "we can solve Johnny's obstinance problem in three sessions," than the kid throws a wrench into the formula by starting some new quirky behavior, and I need to figure out a creative tactic in order to help his parents. That's when I remind myself of the complexities of parenting and how staying one step ahead of our kids can truly be challenging.

Before a baby is born, parents often don't think about all the problems that can occur in raising a child. Planning for a baby can be such fun—picking out names, decorating the nursery, baby showers, and unending anticipation. And then it happens. All the reading, planning, and talking with your friends cannot begin to prepare you for the inevitable mix of excitement, uncertainty, and –yes–physical pain of childbirth. But somehow, no matter how much it hurts to give birth or to watch your wife endure labor, or how adamantly you swear that you will never, ever do this again to yourself, once you hold your baby in your arms, he's instantly the most wonderful and important creature on earth. That's precisely where the irrational part of parenting begins—the kid hasn't done much of anything except peek at you from half-opened eyes, and you belong to him forever. Paternal and maternal instincts kick in, and we wouldn't hesitate to throw ourselves in front of a moving train in order to prove our unconditional love for Junior.

And so the process begins: baby comes home from the hospital and through a variety of information sources—mother, mother-in-law, pediatrician, latest baby book—we do our best to raise our kids. Some of us discuss issues before they occur ("Will we let Junior cry it out or give in and allow him to sleep in our bed?"), while many new parents deal with things as they come up and hope for the best.

I've found that the latter type of parenting is the most common, and the most precarious. If your baby happens to be easygoing (and some are by nature), you'll appear to be a parenting whiz without having to do much at all. However, if you're blessed with a stubborn, bullheaded, "my-way-or-the-highway" kid, no amount of handwringing, finger pointing, or prayer will help. I've found that bullheaded babies abound, and as they grow into toddlers and young children, they become even more determined to have things their way.

But kid behavior can be changed—and I've learned that your attitude toward child rearing greatly determines what type of adult your child will become. Kids are not born with self-discipline, cooperative attitudes, or healthy value systems. They need to be taught these things, and their primary teacher is you—the mother or father.

The trouble is that many kids are not willing students. They do not particularly want to learn to take no for an answer—they want only to hear yes from Mom or Dad. Most don't give a hoot about cleaning up their room or helping you with the laundry. Kids want to have fun, to be given toys, and to do things their way. If their way happens to coincide with your way, things tend to work out. If not, which is often the case, conflict between parent and child occurs. And that's where I come in.

Pediatricians, guidance counselors, teachers, and ministers send families to my office in order to help bring back harmony to chaotic lives by teaching parents how to get a better grip on their children's behavior. In some cases, families come in for what I call a "tune-up"—a minor adjustment of rules here and there, and then they're on their way. Other families, though, are in such turmoil that it's a wonder no one has been hurt. Still others have crossed over the line and abuse has already occurred, with either the parent or child being harmed physically or mentally.

Except for the easy tune-ups, changing the atmosphere in many families can be a challenge. Years of no rules, inconsistent rules, or unfair rules may have prevailed, and the family members have developed various ways of coping, attacking, or defending. Kids have learned to be manipulative in order to gain control, and many parents cave in and let them have their way.

It's easy to fall into this trap, but at some point the conflict between parent and child reaches a level of discomfort where it can no longer be tolerated. Typical of this are my clients Karen and Patrick, and their eight-, eleven-, and fourteen-year-old sons, David, Andrew, and Ryan.

Karen and Patrick were referred to me by David's school guidance counselor. This third grader had recently begun talking back to his teacher and was having trouble getting along with some of his classmates. David liked to tease, but he fell apart when kids began to tease him back. The guidance counselor had tried working with David, but he tended to daydream during their sessions and not participate. At a school conference with David's parents the counselor learned that he and his older brothers were also non-compliant at home. No matter what Karen and Patrick tried—nagging, yelling, and spanking—the kids had to be constantly reminded to complete even the most basic chores. The parents had given up and were doing all of the housework themselves while the boys spent their time playing football or watching TV.

Patrick and Karen were fed up with the situation, but had resigned themselves to several more years of servitude. The guidance counselor, however, was familiar with my style of therapy, called "behavior management," and felt that I could help the parents get back into control.

When they arrived at my office, the boys were curious as to what a "shrink" would be like and what I would have to offer them. After hearing how Karen and Patrick had basically raised the boys by "putting out fires," just dealing with issues as they arose, I suggested starting the *family* on a behavior management system, a program of clear rules and definite consequences for behavior both good and bad. Not only would the boys be involved, but the parents' behavior would be modified in order to change the dynamics of the family.

It took about an hour to come up with the rules and consequences of the behavior management system. The boys were initially a bit wary of the new family rules that we set up, and their parents were not sure that they would actually follow through with the plan.

When we met ten days later we reviewed what worked and what didn't and made changes accordingly. Over the next several weeks, the boys' behavior changed dramatically—they became more responsible and reasonable. Karen and Patrick became more confident in their parenting abilities as they saw that nagging, yelling, and threatening were no longer necessary—a simple behavior management program really worked for their family. As icing on the cake, David's behavior in the classroom improved because he was now receiving a daily consequence at home for his behavior at school.

Karen and Patrick are typical of the parents that I see daily— good people with normal problems whose kids have somehow taken control. That's what this book is all about—teaching folks how to turn their problems around with behavior management. The techniques may initially sound a bit manipulative and per- haps even too simplistic—but they work! I have used behavior management with hundreds of families in my private practice, and thousands of other families are familiar with my system through my seminars, books, and media appearances. It's not uncommon to receive a letter from a thankful parent who can't believe how quickly his family turned around once they followed the system. It's a great feeling to be able to help people in an area so impor- tant to our lives—our families. And this book will be able to help yours if you can accept that kids need guidelines and that you, the parent, are the one to develop and enforce them.

This book is written for *all* families of kids ages seven to six- teen. It will work if your family is happy yet disorganized, or if the kids must be nagged constantly to complete chores. It will even work if the kids are running the show and the parents have prac- tically given up on discipline. And it's also for those folks in fam- ilies that are running smoothly who wish to continue to do so for many years to come. Before I show you how to design a behavior management system for your specific family needs in Chapter 6, you'll learn about the parenting styles that work and don't work, the types of kids who love to push our parenting buttons, and some disciplinary ground rules that are important.

My own kids have grown up with a behavior management system as part of their lives. The system I use changes and evolves as they grow older, but the realization that their behavior leads to clear and definite consequences has helped my children to usually make the right choices and decisions. Of course there are occasional "blips" on the screen, but they've turned out to be terrific kids who abide by our rules.

And this, I believe, is the basis of raising good children. Kids who learn to accept and to expect defined consequences for their behavior (for example, if you make good grades, you can have more privileges) understand the concept of personal responsibility. It makes sense to them, and they do not see a need to defy or avoid responsible behavior as adults. They adjust to society's values and learn to accept that one doesn't always get one's way—a value that becomes very important later in social and work situations. In essence, they learn to become reasonable and rational— but they must learn these lessons from you, their parent.

This type of parenting is not always an easy road to follow, and there have been many times when it's taken all of my creativity and tenacity to outsmart a strong-willed manipulative child. But in the end it's worth it.

As I began with the admission that I definitely do not know everything about child rearing, I end with the conviction that I do know at least one thing for sure. Kids grow up to be the adults we, as parents, mold them to be. Their values and ethics mimic ours. Your children are watching how you live, how you make decisions, and how you respond to their behaviors. It may be an overwhelming feeling knowing that not only are you responsible for yourself, but also for teaching appropriate values to the children you bring into this world.

Remember, from the moment that little guy peeks at you with half-opened eyes in the delivery room, he's watching and learning from you—his parent, his teacher.

CHALLENGING KIDS

Lying . . . refusing to do as told . . . talking back . . . not taking no for an answer . . . being disrespectful to authority . . . and the list went on. That is how Sam and Connie described the behavior of their eleven-year-old daughter, Jenny, at our first therapy session together. When I read the list aloud, Jenny, dressed in soccer shorts and a T-shirt, grinned defiantly and nodded her head. She agreed that her behavior had been awful lately, and she almost seemed to be proud of it.

Connie was at her wit's end and Sam admitted that he had recently considered spanking his daughter, and that's why they felt therapy was necessary. Jenny's attitude had become a mixture of cockiness and disrespect, and her folks had to ask her several times to do any chore before she begrudgingly complied. For example, they had to nag her to take the dog out for a walk or to put her dirty clothes in the hamper. Sam and Connie felt defeated as parents. No matter how they approached her, Jenny seemed determined to give them a hard time. She tantrummed when her needs were not immediately met, and her folks felt as if they were walking on eggshells around her.

"It wasn't always like this," noted Connie. "Sure, Jenny was always a stubborn kid who wanted her way, but at a younger age she would usually give in." After listening to Jenny's history I noted to

Sam and Connie that Jenny had moved from being a willful but compliant child to a bratty preteen. They agreed with this and committed to a series of therapy sessions teaching them how to get their child's behavior back on track.

When Parents Can't Say No

Day after day I see families like Jenny's, with kids ranging in age from two through adolescence who are determined not to comply with parental requests. Generally the kids are grumpy, whiny, or obnoxious—unconcerned with how their insensitive and selfish behaviors affect their families. Over the years as I've worked with families struggling to regain harmony, I've noticed that this pattern appears to be growing.

And I'm not alone in this observation. Psychologists have had the opportunity for more than four decades to view a very disturbing trend in children's behavior. More and more kids appear to be lacking in self-control, are egocentric, and display poor frustration tolerance. Being able to delay gratification and accept that at times the world may be unfair helps them become prepared for the frustrating events that inevitably happen to all of us throughout our lives.

Why are parents today so conflicted about limit setting and discipline? I believe that it is based in ineffective parental training. Over the past forty years many psychologists, pediatricians, and child care workers have taught parents to view conflicts with their children merely as differences of opinion and misunderstandings. These child-rearing experts have proposed that using discipline to teach may even be harmful, and therefore reasoning, understanding, and discussing have become the mainstays of discipline. This laissez-faire attitude asks parents to allow "natural consequences" to affect their children. In her book *Reviving Ophelia: Saving the Souls of Adolescent Girls,* Mary Pipher recounts the story of a mother who actually had *parenting* confused with *abuse.* The mother "was trying so hard to be good to her daughter that she was denying her the chance to grow up." Pipher told the mother that she was in danger of "understanding her daughter all the way into juvenile court." In effect, parents have been taught to try to "reason with the unreasonable." Young children tend to be egocentric and normally have not yet developed the ability to see things from others' perspectives.

In the classic book *The New Dare to Discipline,* James Dobson reports that parents have been told that a child "will eventually respond to reason and forbearance, ruling out the need for discipline. . . ." Parents have been told to "encourage the child's rebellion because it offered a valuable release of hostility." According to Dobson, some experts recommend that parents verbalize or reflect the child's feelings when she is upset, such as saying, "You want the water, but you're angry because I brought it too late," as the child is dumping the water on the ground. But emotional reflection does little to teach the youngster better behavior and may actually promote poor frustration tolerance.

In this atmosphere of disciplinary uncertainty, is it any wonder that parents today are confused? In his book *Touchpoints: Your Child's Emotional and Behavioral Development,* Dr. T. Berry Brazelton says that "when both parents are away at work all day, they hate to be disciplinarians in their limited time at home. But children will save their provocative behavior all day to try it out in a safe, loving environment." Not wanting to discipline their kids because of guilt feelings or fear of conflict, many folks then simply disengage themselves from the parenting role. But sooner or later, these parents may begin to feel as if they are being held hostage by their own children.

It's interesting that toasters, CD players, and Lego sets come with complex instructions in at least two languages, but our most precious new acquisition, a baby, does not. We go to Lamaze class for pain preparation and consult an interior decorator for designing baby's room, yet how many prospective parents actively put even one-tenth of their prebaby time and budget into learning about child care and development? We spend hours poring over baby name books, agonizing over the psychological effects of naming our son Michael versus Jason, but allow little to no time discussing some disciplinary tactics. Parents have specific ideas about how they want their children to *be*—motivated in school, respectful to adults, sensitive and caring—but they do not often focus on the day-to-day specifics of their child's behavior until they find that one day Junior has taken over the family.

The Consequence of No Consequences

Childhood is the training ground for later adult behavior. The lessons parents teach their children, both purposefully and inadvertently, are long lasting and color their children's future adult actions and temperament. It is the parents' job to teach the child. Kids will change their behaviors when their parents change their expectations. If a parent expects a child to develop consistent self-control by middle school, the child will do so if the stage is set at an early age.

Children with self-control will develop into adults who are self-disciplined and productive. It is the exceptional young adult who has led a chaotic adolescence with little parental guidance who then "sees the light," finishes high school and college, and becomes successful. There are individuals among us like that. However, the majority of these kids evolve into irresponsible adults, because these seeds were planted in their early years.

In his book *The Road Less Traveled: A New Psychology of Love, Traditional Values, and Spiritual Growth,* Dr. M. Scott Peck notes that "discipline is the basic set of tools we require to solve life's problems. Without discipline we can solve nothing, and with some discipline we can solve only some problems. With total discipline we can solve all problems." Youngsters who were taught self-control at an early age often were exposed to disciplinary tactics by their parents as a natural part of the developmental process. These kids generally develop and understand self-discipline naturally as adults. Most likely they will also pass this gift on to their own kids, perpetuating a positive approach to disciplining children.

But when parents are themselves undisciplined and therefore offer poor role models for their children, the tools for the development of self-control are not passed on to the next generation, and irresponsible values and impulsivity are transferred from parent to child. This impulsive, irresponsible lifestyle will follow the children into and through adulthood. Breaking the cycle of low frustration tolerance, irresponsibility, and self-indulgence is a must if the next generation is to succeed.

Parents cannot look to educators, ministers, or pediatricians to teach their children responsibility and self-discipline. It must come from the home environment. Consistent, well-disciplined parents are the prescription for the evolution of self-disciplined successful youngsters. Families in which children are in charge are chaotic, unpleasant environments for all—parents, kids, relatives, friends, neighbors, and even complete strangers who end up drawn into a family drama. Kids are happier and more self-confident when they know the rules and realize that they can live within the guidelines.

How Parents Lose Control

It is interesting how kids come to control a family. Most parents have very good intentions. They love their children and will give them everything they can. They give in the material sense and in terms of time and attention. The process seems to go awry, however, when the parent gives to the child *unconditionally.* Parents tend to reward youngsters inadvertently for very inappropriate behaviors.

For example, the teenager who continues to harass his folks to let him use the car even though his grades have been poor is all too typical. His father may have already established the rule that he will not be able to drive until he has achieved at least a C average in school. But before he has accomplished this the teen may have manipulated Dad into letting him use the car "just one more time." In this case, unconditional reward only serves to teach the child the inappropriate lesson that harassing and manipulating achieve one's goals.

Caring parents often *want* to give children unconditional rewards—whatever they can afford to give. In addition, unconditional rewards are often used in an effort to avoid conflict. Most parents do not enjoy getting into arguments with their kids and tend to take the easy way out. This usually means giving in to the child, which results in gaining the immediate goal. It is obvious, however, that unconditional rewards are not in the youngster's long-term best interest. The real world will not often give in to temper tantrums and demanding behavior.

Thus the child may grow up without learning tactics to deal with frustration. Youngsters who do not learn how to take no for an answer tend to become adolescents who are impulsive and irresponsible. Instead of attending a boring class, impulsive kids tend to skip school to do something that is more fun. All too often they end up in juvenile court being lectured by a judge about responsibility. As adults it's nearly impossible for them to stay at a job because a promotion may be years away, or to learn new behaviors in order to save a marriage. These kids are often seen later as individuals with unstable work patterns and marital problems.

As parents, we tend to avoid dealing with conflict because our kids often make us feel guilty when things do not go their way. We ask ourselves, "What would our parents have done in this situation?" or "What will the effect be on my child if I do not allow him to have what he is asking for or to do what he wants to do?" In an effort to do the best job that we can, parents often give their children too much. *Too much* includes too many material objects, too many freedoms, and too much control over others. In the process of giving our kids too much, we are not teaching them enough of a very important skill—self-control. The issues of self-control, responsibility, and frustration tolerance are integral parts of an effective child-rearing program.

PARENTING STYLES:
Why We Parent the Way We Do

Every one of us was raised by an authority figure of some sort—birth parent, stepparent, adoptive parent, foster parent, orphanage, or grandmother—so we all have had the opportunity to come into contact with at least one parenting style. Parents differ tremendously in disciplinary tactics—some are militaristic and others laissez-faire, while some flip-flop between the two depending upon how things went at the office that day.

I've found that the least effective parenting style is the parent who is *consistently inconsistent*—changing tactics, demands, and consequences to meet his or her own immediate needs and moods. These parents tend to confuse their kids, leading either to frightened children who must constantly tread on thin ice around their folks, or else to manipulative children who use guilt tactics to convince the inconsistent parent how unfair she is, thereby avoiding any consequences for their own behavior.

How do parents develop their individual disciplinary styles? Many, I'm convinced, don't think ahead; they just fall into whatever seems to work at the moment. They use a mixture of one part talk-show guru suggestion, two parts mother and mother-in-law input, and a bit of what the nosy neighbor next door throws in. Of course their child is a mess. Who wouldn't be when there is no well-thought-out disciplinary plan?

I believe that new parents don't discuss discipline early on because they feel that it won't come into play before the child's second birthday. Are they ever wrong! Discipline needs to start in the baby's first few months of life, when structure should become a part of the daily routine in the form of naps, feeding, and bedtime.

Parents also tend to make decisions about discipline, consequences, and consistency based upon their own childhood experiences. If your folks were militaristic and it worked, you might try the same tactics. If you grew up resenting that strictness and fell into a rebellious stage, you probably will try the opposite tack. Too often, we swing 180 degrees from our childhood experience. The bitter child of militaristic parents becomes a wishy-washy father. The wandering child of laissez-faire folks may parent like Attila the Hun, often overreacting and enforcing rules that are just not necessary.

You'll know that your disciplinary tactics are off base by watching your kids' reactions to them. If your kids show you a lack of respect, you're probably tolerating too much inappropriate behavior. If, on the other hand, they appear to be fearful of you, then you're probably too strict. These are red flags that you have overdone a parenting tactic. Try a more compromised approach, one that meets your needs as a parent as well as your child's.

Look at your own family situation. Are your kids pretty reasonable? Do they listen well? Does your spouse back you up when you've made a command decision? If the answer is yes, then perhaps your family will thrive on a middle-of-the-road approach—important rules prevail, but let the little stuff go and give a warning instead of an immediate consequence for infractions. But if your kids are becoming discipline problems, you need to step back and analyze your parenting style.

• • •

The Cardinal Rules for Parenting

I will discuss the various parenting styles in this chapter and later present what style I feel to be the most effective. But regardless of the parenting style you use, there are two cardinal rules for disciplining kids:

1. *Be consistent (this can't be said enough).*

2. *Take a cool, calm, and almost nonchalant attitude when giving out consequences. A screaming, red-faced parent is often quite amusing to a kid.*

Let's look at consistency first. Stephanie, a forty-two-year-old single parent and owner of a beauty salon, complained to me that her fifteen-year-old daughter, Lisa, was "out of control." Lisa wouldn't listen to her, talked back incessantly, and refused to follow her mother's rules, few as they were. Eventually, to show her mother who was really the boss, Lisa moved in with a girlfriend and her family, and Stephanie gave in and allowed her to do so.

Stephanie was what I refer to as a hand wringer. She nagged Lisa and threatened her with punishment if the few chores she assigned weren't done or curfew was broken. But for all the yakking she did, Stephanie rarely took action. Why? Because she wanted to be Lisa's friend and buddy. Stephanie's parents had been rigid and dictatorial with her, and she swore that she would be more fair with her own child. The lesson Lisa learned was that nothing major was going to happen to her if she disobeyed her mother. She could tune out Mom's nagging and lecturing, and both of them ended up bitter, feeling as if they were victims of each other's selfishness.

Stephanie blamed Lisa's uninvolved father, her errant friends, and most of all "the system." She asked me, "Why is nobody doing anything to help straighten out this kid?" Well, the buck stops with the parent. Stephanie had trouble standing up to her daughter, confronting her, and setting limits and consequences when she disobeyed. It was easier for Stephanie to give in and become the victim of Lisa's inappropriate behavior.

Why would a mother allow this to happen? To put it simply, Stephanie had already lost her husband's love and couldn't bear the possibility of losing her daughter's love as well. When I suggested this to her, she listened, cried, admitted it was true, and quickly went back to playing the victim role ("But why can't Lisa just see that I'm hurting?").

Lisa couldn't see it because she had always been allowed to ignore the consequences her actions had on her mother, and on other people, too. She actually had been trained to be selfish and self-centered, so how could she even begin to understand the depth of her mother's feelings? I wish I could say that there was a happy ending to this encounter, but they discontinued therapy prematurely. Had Stephanie been able to endure Lisa's anger and resentment for a few weeks while she learned to set limits and to use fair consequences, the kid would have been able to learn trust, liking, love, and most important, respect for her mom.

Although they won't admit it, kids want limits, because limits in the home often provide the only security that children experience. Kids need predictability—they need to know what's going to happen next, what positive consequences will occur if they work hard, and what discomfort they will have to endure if they slack off. Parents who are on opposite ends of the spectrum—either overpermissive or irrationally strict—cause children to guess at the consequences of their behavior.

And don't forget the calm, nonchalant attitude mentioned above as a cardinal rule—even the best consequence can be ruined if the parent falls into a screaming meltdown! Many kids I speak to in my practice report that they actually wait until Mom or Dad is screaming at them before they take the parental request seriously. It's as if a certain decibel level has to be reached before the switch is turned on and the child actually listens. Too often Mom or Dad is so mad by then that the punishment is inappropriate—leaping from nagging to hard smacking or threatening ridiculous punishments that everyone knows will not be used.

To state it simply: Consequences need to be immediate, important to the child, predictable, and calmly given. Rules that lead to consequences should be clear, jointly determined by both parent and child, and fair. So, if you find yourself constantly reasoning, cajoling, nagging, yelling, and reminding your child to complete tasks or decrease a certain obnoxious behavior, quit beating a dead horse and learn some new tactics. It's time for action, and your child *will* respond.

Quiz Time

I bet some of you are wondering whether you need to change your parenting style. Well, it's time for a short quiz. Be honest when answering these questions. You'll know that you are trying to "reason with the unreasonable" instead of disciplining your child appropriately if you answer yes to most of the following items:

1. You wonder why you can't just be your child's friend (buddy, chum) and not have to force him to do things he doesn't want to do.

2. You flash back to how you were raised, and the word "discipline" sends chills down your spine. You vowed to give your kids negative consequences only as a last resort, if ever.

3. You argue constantly with your spouse, who wants to put your son in time-out or remove a privilege for misbehavior. You feel there is nothing wrong with constantly having to remind your son to complete a chore because, well, "boys will be boys."

4. You've never really been strict and consistent in your own life—and the thought of setting up rules and actually having to follow through with them is very frightening. You're more worried about your own failure to use a system of rules than about your child's ability to succeed.

5. You've tried everything—time-out, taking away privileges, spankings— and nothing seems to work. The problem is, you tend to skip from one consequence to another without giving each one sufficient time to have an effect on your child.

6. You suffer more than your child does when she is grounded. It infringes upon your freedom, and you're not willing to make the sacrifice.

7. You're afraid your child will hate you if you make him lose out on a privilege. You believe this feeling toward you will be permanent.

8. Your spouse overreacts and punishes too quickly, so you feel that you must play the "buffer" and be lenient on your child. This way your kid experiences either leniency or abuse but rarely a compromised, reasonable position.

9. You feel used, manipulated, and powerless after discussing an inappropriate behavior with your kid for the umpteenth time, but he seems so sincere, and those big eyes make you melt and give in.

10. You want to leave. Who asked for these darned kids to begin with?

If you admit to many of these behaviors and feelings, you're probably not parenting as effectively as you could. You may be like Stephanie, an *emotionally needy* parent who wants her daughter to be her buddy, or you may find yourself to be a *happiness seeker,* or a *wait-'til-your-father-gets-home* parent. First, let's look at others like Stephanie, who seek adult comfort from their children.

The Emotionally Needy Parent

One of the most heartbreaking of ineffective parenting styles is that of the *emotionally needy* parent. Often these are single parents or those who stay married even though they are unhappy in the relationship. It's amazing how many parents are lonely and miserable in their marriages. For a variety of good and not-so-good reasons, they stick it out. "We're staying together for the kids" is probably the most common reason given. Have you heard the one about the eighty-two-year-old husband and his eighty-year-old wife? Married fifty-three miserable years, parents of four kids, and when asked why they had never divorced, Mama says, "We've talked about it many times but are waiting for the kids to die first."

Miserable spouses often look to other avenues for support and distraction. Some focus too much on their jobs and become workaholics, others overeat and become food addicts, and many lonely souls seek comfort from their kids. All are normal reactions to unhappy situations.

However, when you lose the balance between working a bit too hard and working all of the time, eating constantly even though it's unhealthy and you really don't feel hungry, and using your child for the emotional support that you should be getting from your spouse, something is out of whack and somebody usually gets hurt.

Many parents have confessed to me how much they depend upon their kids to give meaning to their lives or to have someone to talk to. Some seek their kids' advice on all types of issues—especially marital ones. As Becky, a client in my practice, explained: "I can't get any response from my husband, so I tell my ten-year-old son my problems, including how I feel about his dad. I know I shouldn't, but David sees how his father treats me and knows how lonely I've become. It really helps that someone in this family understands what I'm going through."

Sounds innocent enough on the surface, perhaps, but what Becky is laying on David is way beyond what he can handle. Perhaps this pattern keeps Becky sane, but it sure is messing with young David's emotional health. He told me that he's caught between feelings for his victim mother and seemingly uninvolved father, with no place to go himself. I don't expect a ten-year-old to convince Dad to change his ways, and David feels too guilty to tell his mom to stop dumping her problems on him. In addition, David noted that he feels quite uncomfortable when he is with both parents at the same time. He can sense their tension and feels guilty and disloyal if he is nice to Dad when Mom is around.

I warned Becky that as the years go on, the boundary between parent and child will disappear. At fifteen David will no longer feel that he should ask permission to do what he wants—he'll tell his mother what he's going to do rather than ask. Having grown up as her emotional peer, he'll see no reason to treat her as a parent—it's more logical to view Mom as an equal. All is okay as long as David and Mom are on the same wavelength, but as soon as he wants to follow his own ideas and overrule her judgment, the trouble will begin. You can't have one set of rules when it's convenient for you ("We're buddies, let me share my problems with you"), and another set when you decide to take control ("I'm your mother and you will not stay out past midnight"). It's not fair, it's unpredictable, and it just doesn't work.

Kids who are used as confidants are often conflicted. They feel proud that you treat and speak to them as equals, but resent it when you pull the authority gig (on a whim, as they often see it). I'm not suggesting that you shouldn't share emotions with your kids—feelings, both good and bad, are part of daily life. It's the sharing of adult conflicts such as marital issues that place the child in the awkward position of constantly hearing negative things about one parent from the other.

Many single parents inadvertently share the fears and insecurities of the single world with the child. These folks tend to place a great deal of emotional responsibility on their kids. Excess emotional baggage that the parent shares with (or dumps on) the child can often do considerable damage. Too often parents realize this too late, after the teen has already begun to establish a pattern of rebellion. Both parties suffer. These parents feel abandoned and used, mourning for the former closeness they shared with their child. The kid, confused as to how a previously equal relationship turned into a dictatorship seemingly overnight, becomes bitter and resentful.

Of course the solution is to avoid the confusion to begin with. No matter how tempting it is to confide your adult problems to your children, the risks are too great. Kids are not your emotional or social equals—they are kids, and that's that. In her book *Dr. Sylvia Rimm's Smart Parenting,* Dr. Rimm discusses the development of thought in children. She warns parents against making the assumption that "children have developed cognitively and morally to an adult level. . . . They are not yet capable of adult thinking." Children have not had enough life experience to understand and deal with the complexities of many adult relationships, especially marriage. It's difficult for them to understand how you can be so unforgiving toward your ex-spouse—after all, it's their mother or father you're complaining about. To expect a child to understand marital stress that even you can't figure out, or to cope with your loneliness following separation or divorce, is unfair and just too stressful for any kid to handle.

In addition, to expect that a youngster who supports you and constantly shares your thoughts and feelings will be able to subjugate himself to your newfound rules when he reaches adolescence is unreasonable. Most kids I've worked with who have had the rug pulled out from under them in this way tend to disrespect the parent and may choose to leave home at an early age. They've grown to feel independent and capable of making adult decisions, because they have for years, and rebel against the parent's new rules, which they feel treat them as children. Also, you've set up an almost impossible situation for the future if you choose to remarry. The stepparent, who will be vying with your child for your affection, will have a great deal of difficulty disciplining your kid and dealing with his old and new resentments.

If you've become an emotionally needy parent, it's time to reevaluate your home situation. Have a talk with your child and tell her that you're not going to dump your adult problems and feelings on her anymore. Discuss rules and responsibilities—yours as the adult as well as hers as the child.

Quiz Time

You will know that you are muddying the parent-child boundary and becoming an emotionally needy parent if:

1. You're lonely and feel that you can't communicate with your spouse. You seldom express your true feelings to him or her, and you think that "keeping the peace is good enough."

2. You often bad-mouth your spouse to your son, without regard to how it will affect his relationship with his father.

3. Your friends don't seem to be as supportive as they used to be when you complained about your home situation.

4. You are more comfortable doing things with your child than with the whole family—you feel more free to talk.

5. You share private matters with your daughter, even though you have a feeling that it may be inappropriate to discuss them with her.

6. Your daughter seems nervous when both you and your spouse are together with her. She prefers to be with each of you separately.

7. Subtle changes are occurring in your relationship with your son. He is beginning to make decisions that you previously took responsibility for.

8. You're finding that the child who was your buddy at age ten no longer respects your wishes at age fifteen. He's acting cocky, and rudely informs you that you can't tell him what to do anymore.

9. You never seemed to need to set house rules before. As a trade-off for confiding in your child you also catered to her whims. Now, if you say no, she becomes enraged.

10. You find yourself becoming concerned that your child may hurt you. The last few times you've tried grounding her for disobeying she has either run out of the house or has raised her hand to you. You fear that she may become aggressive the next time you cross her.

The Happiness-Seeking Parent

Happiness-seeking parents' primary purpose is to make their child as happy as possible. I've learned, however, that the best way to ensure that your daughter will be miserable and unhappy as an adult is for you to totally focus on her happiness as a child. Sound a little nutty? What else would you want for your kid except her happiness? After years of experience I have come to realize that parents who try to make their children happy are not only spinning their wheels, they are actually interfering with their child's healthy development.

How does the pursuit of kid happiness mess up your child? First, no one (not even you) can make your youngster happy. Comfort, pleasure, and good self-esteem are the roots of happiness and contentment, and no one can artificially inject these qualities into another human being. Yet, no matter how much you give to your son, love him, and shower him with things, self-content can still be elusive. Happiness is based in how your child feels about himself and how others feel about him, realizing that he is a good person, and developing self-control so that he can tolerate the frustrating situations that will inevitably crop up in his life as he grows and matures.

My clinical practice is limited to kids and their folks, and almost daily I encounter the *happiness seeker* syndrome: "My kid is going to be happy at any cost, and I am responsible for his happiness." Ten years ago, happiness seekers tended to be yuppies who were determined not to make a single mistake raising their children. However, it seems that this trend has generalized to parents of all socioeconomic status—almost as a disease spreads insidiously. These parents read magazines, watch news coverage, and are glued to talk shows that focus on the "negative adult remnants of early childhood parenting mistakes." The media have made them afraid to stand up to their own kids.

Typical of the happiness seekers are my clients Bob, Laura, and their nine- and thirteen-year-old daughters, Ashley and Danielle. They are middle-class folks—Bob is an accountant and Laura is a preschool teacher. Regular people, decent work ethic, complete with the guilt that most families experience when both parents are working. They continually worry whether they are giving enough attention, time, and stuff to their two children.

Ashley collects Barbie dolls and character toys from fast-food restaurants, loves to play Nintendo, and has tons of energy. She also shows distinct displeasure when her needs are not met immediately. She flies into a temper tantrum, which is generally reinforced when her parents give in to whatever it was that she initially demanded. Ashley, therefore, has actually been trained to throw temper tantrums and has developed a very low frustration tolerance.

Danielle has just had her thirteenth birthday, and received lots of gifts from friends and family, but valued very few of them. Mom and Dad also made sure that there was a gift for Ashley so that she wouldn't feel left out and unhappy.

Bob and Laura work very hard to keep their kids comfortable and well stocked with the latest toys, gadgets, and gizmos. What has them stymied, though, is that both girls seem to tire quickly of their possessions, becoming moody and dissatisfied. This is the opposite of what their parents expected to happen when they provided for both of the girls' desires.

In therapy, I counseled Bob and Laura to give their daughters adequate time and attention, but to make Danielle and Ashley earn their toys and privileges. No more receiving an allowance on Saturday morning just for showing up alive; the girls were now taught how to work for their rewards. They also learned emotional self-control when their desires were not immediately met by receiving negative consequences for tantrumming.

The parents were taught that a little bit of indulgence can be a good thing, but a child raised on a steady diet of "me as the center of the universe" is generally quite harmful. Why? Because Danielle and Ashley are not the center of the universe and never will be. Better their parents prepare them for the reality of having to share and, yes, even to experience disappointment and unhappiness. This is not to say that unhappy events should be promoted and planned by parents, but rather that children should not be protected from everyday disappointments. Unpleasantness, peer rejection, and self-consciousness are part of the stuff of growing up, and kids who are sheltered from the realities of childhood as well as the responsibilities of maturation often grow up to be bitter, irresponsible adults who never quite adjust to society's demands. Children who are raised with a feeling of entitlement become easily depressed as teenagers and adults when their peers refuse to cater to their whims. Adult temper tantrums are scorned by others, and Mom and Dad can no longer make the world a rosy place.

I believe that it was much harder for Bob and Laura to change their behavior than for the girls to adjust to the new rules. They occasionally still felt guilty when saying no to their kids, and old tapes of their own childhoods still ran through their minds. Bob's folks had been overly strict, and he remembered having been afraid to discuss his true feelings with them, as he feared they would interpret his disagreement as argumentative. Laura's mother let her run the show and spoiled her materially in an effort to make up for her husband's lack of involvement with the kids. These childhood memories made Laura and Bob try hard not to disappoint their own kids, but they soon realized that the girls would survive not being catered to.

Danielle and Ashley quickly responded better to their parents once their immediate happiness was not the focus of their parents' lives. The girls' behavior and character became the barometer of success.

I'm not suggesting that this type of change is easy. Changing parenting styles can be quite tough. In fact, it can be downright awful. But even more disheartening is the realization later in your child's life that your adorable, overindulged little one has grown into a selfish, insecure, and unprepared adult. Do not focus on winning the battle (immediate kid satisfaction) while losing the war (adult happiness and self-respect). Children who are catered to often become so egocentric that they cannot place themselves in others' shoes and are, therefore, often labeled as insensitive and selfish. Peers soon learn to avoid them, considering the child a nuisance or an irritant. Surely not the recipe for happiness that the parents of the indulged child planned for!

Happiness, it seems, is the result of good parenting. You cannot buy it, fake it, talk your child into it, or manipulate the world to provide it. Happiness is a state of comfort that develops when you are content with your relationships with others, having developed a healthy balance between fulfilling your own needs while helping others with theirs. It is the security of knowing that your child can control his emotions and behavior so that no matter what challenges he faces, he can act appropriately. Spoiled, entitled children rarely rise to this level of character, and they forever pay for their parents' indulgence.

Think about it—it's never too late to start setting limits, to say no to unreasonable requests, and to begin to build your child's character in a healthy way. In his provocative book *Emotional Intelligence,* Daniel Goleman provides statistics from several studies showing that parents who are involved and who set consistent guidelines for their children are rewarded with young adults who have developed "a set of traits—some call it character—that also matter immensely for our personal destiny." And studies show that most people who develop good character also enjoy positive self-esteem, are well liked by others, and, yes, *turn out to be very happy.*

Quiz Time

Happiness seeking is an easy trap to fall into, but one that you can avoid by better understanding your feelings and motivations as a parent. Check it out in your home. If you see yourself in the following items, you may be a happiness-seeking parent.

1. You give in to your child because you can't bear to see her unhappy (sad, miserable, hurting).

2. You distort the truth so that your kid feels good about herself at the expense of not understanding reality. ("Mary doesn't call you anymore because there is something wrong with Mary. The fights between you two have absolutely nothing to do with what you did.")

3. You are unable to criticize your youngster because you fear you will damage his self-esteem, even at the cost of not helping him to correct character flaws that will cause him problems later in his life.

4. You rush to fill your child's every wish because he is sad, mad, or unhappy, and because you become upset when he is frustrated.

5. You feel guilty or that you are a bad or ineffective parent when your child doesn't agree with your decisions.

6. You feel that you, as the parent, have the power, ability, and responsibility to cure your kid's peer arguments and friend problems.

7. You dread your child's moodiness when she doesn't get her way. You avoid saying no to her because you just don't want to deal with the fallout.

8. You often walk on eggshells around your kids.

9. You generally put your needs behind your child's whims—even if he doesn't seem to notice or appreciate what you do for him.

10. You were not a happy child, and you vowed never to let upsetting things happen to your kids.

The Wait-'Til-Your-Father-Gets-Home Parent

The *wait-'til-your-father-gets-home* parent is another frequent visitor to my office. This style is actually a double dose of bad parenting. First, the "waiting" part is precarious because discipline should occur as soon as possible after the infraction, and second, parents need to present a united front while doling out the consequences for inappropriate behavior.

Although I've seen some "wait-'til-your-mother-gets-home" situations, most kids I've worked with tend to take their fathers more seriously than their mothers. It may be the deeper voice, or the fact that Junior is already as tall as Mom, but it's a fairly consistent pattern. Surprisingly, most kids who respond better for their fathers than for their mothers do not report doing so because Dad spanks harder than Mom—in fact, most of these families do not use corporal punishment.

Many families go through a period of life without a father in the home, or if Dad is available he may work late hours and not be able to be "Johnny on the spot" at five o'clock when Mom would like him to set the kids straight. My clients Marilyn and Michael are a good example of this. A thirty-nine-year-old mother of three (ages seven, twelve, and fourteen), Marilyn looks at least ten years older than she actually is, with frown lines and hands she wrings constantly. Michael is a long-distance trucker who travels frequently, and Marilyn is in charge of the three kids while he is gone. Michael dreads his semiweekly calls home because everyone whines and complains. Marilyn feels helpless and spends their conversations relaying a laundry list of each kid's crimes—not doing as told when told, arguing with siblings—and the children use their phone time with their dad to tattle on each other. Michael often accuses Marilyn of being an incompetent parent because it seems that she can't handle the kids when he isn't there. Not a very pleasant situation for anyone, as is often the case when the kids are out of control.

During therapy Michael made the point that he had to make a living, and long-haul trucking provided the most money for his family. He depends upon Marilyn to run the home when he's gone. Both parents are frustrated, angry with each other as well as with the kids. Marilyn needs to learn to take control of the children as issues occur, so that she will not have to resort to the wait-'til-your-father-gets-home tactic that she habitually uses. Michael needs to develop faith in her parenting ability so that when he calls home he doesn't get suckered into playing judge and jury. He needs to back up his wife and to let the kids know that her decision is final, especially when he is out of town.

I firmly suggested that the family receive behavior management counseling to achieve these goals. I knew they could do it once they learned how to set up clear guidelines, and I showed Marilyn how to use effective parenting skills. It took several therapy sessions because Marilyn was so used to passing the buck to Michael, but she finally learned to stand her ground with the kids and to handle their misbehavior herself.

The message I give to wait-'til-your-father-gets-home parents is that your kid needs to learn to respect *you* and to comply with *your* wishes. Children who have a bit of a "healthy fear" of their parents tend to be good kids. Many folks think I'm a few screws short when I suggest that a child who fears his parents is a healthy child. What I mean by "healthy fear" is the child thinking, "If I disobey, Mom will notice and will do something that I don't like [such as a negative consequence]. She's not going to beat me or scream or nag at me for hours. She'll take away my daily allowance, or I'll lose TV, or I'll be grounded or my curfew will be made earlier. Each of these is a pretty tough consequence individually, but if she uses all of them, it will really hurt. Maybe I'd be better off doing what she wants in the first place."

That's what I mean by setting up "healthy fear." It's definitely not fear of being physically or emotionally hurt by a parent. It's your child's realistic concern that you, as a parent, will actually give negative consequences for her negative behaviors. Pretty scary thought for a kid, and it really works if you've been consistent and have set up a plan of action. Even if you're only 80 percent consistent, your kid will become a believer.

Healthy fear leads to healthy respect. I see it happen all of the time in my practice. Try an experiment—ask your friends. When they were growing up, who was the "heavy" in their family? Many will say it was their father. And if he used healthy consequences (not beatings, cursing, or ridiculous punishments), most of your friends will add that they listened to him, either because they respected him or because they didn't want to find out what would happen if they didn't follow Dad's requests. Many probably will report that they also respected their mothers—again, because Mom (perhaps in a gentler way) stood her ground, and they knew that if they ever wanted to be released from grounding or restrictions, then they had better mind their manners.

Another group will note that they loved their mother but didn't particularly respect her, and also felt sorry for Mom because she couldn't seem to control the kids. Or that they feared their father and didn't respect him, but actually hated him. These types of families were those in which the wait-'til-your-father-gets-home threat was liberally used, Mom was not taken seriously, and Dad was feared because when he did get home, inappropriate and often harsh consequences were given. Kids were beaten, cursed at, or actually thrown out of the house. This type of situation does not foster respect; it evolves into pity and disrespect for Mom (and still little compliance from the child, by the way) and hatred for Dad.

And it's not fair to either parent. Mom feels that her hands are tied, and Dad feels used. He's so busy punishing that it's almost impossible for him to develop a good relationship with his children. And after a while, these patterns become so ingrained that these disciplinary tactics actually become bad habits, behaviors used even though they are ineffective.

Why do folks become victim to this parenting style? Partly because kids can drive you so nuts that if you don't have a reasonable behavior management system ready to use at your fingertips, you just react. Passive parents become hostages to their tyrannical kids, and aggressive parents bypass reasonable compromises and leap to intimidation and abuse. Neither of these styles leads to respect. The kids end up pitying or ignoring the weak parent and feeling a great deal of bitterness and resentment toward the frightening one.

If this scenario sounds all too familiar to you, why not just stop the cycle right now? Commit to taking some risks, such as using a behavior management system of rules and limit setting. Kids who are about 80 percent sure of the consequences of their actions—because no parent is 100 percent consistent all of the time—respect their parents, even if it means disliking the consequence.

The old jingle "a little dab'll do ya" really fits here—just a small amount of healthy fear of an appropriate, humane, and predictable consequence goes a long way. And as a bonus, when Dad doesn't have to come home to a disastrous situation that he must handle, he'll tend to be calmer and more pleasant, and he'll actually have the opportunity to develop good relationships with his kids. I realize that often it's easier to continue with an ineffective old pattern than to try a potentially successful new behavior. New things tend to frighten us, and fear is something we like to avoid. However, there are big stakes at risk here, folks, and I think the payoff is worth the risk.

Quiz Time

You're falling into the wait-'til-your-father-gets-home trap if:

1. You literally use that phrase at least three times a week.
2. Your spouse travels and you dread the days he is gone, not so much because you miss him, but because of the way the kids take advantage of you when he's away.
3. Your spouse is annoyed with your phone calls at work because you're not handling the problems at home, and he thinks that you're an incompetent parent.

4. Even you are beginning to think that you're incompetent as a parent—or at least ineffective.

5. The kids show their dad respect, but don't seem to appreciate what you do for them.

6. You're contemplating going to work and hiring a sitter so that you don't have to be the one to discipline the children from nine to five.

7. Your parents were harsh with you and your siblings, and you have vowed to give your kids the benefit of the doubt and not punish if possible.

8. Friends tell you to be tougher with the kids, but you ignore their advice because they don't have to live with your children; they "just don't understand."

9. Your husband complains that he feels used—all he's there for is to discipline, and there's little time for fun with the children.

10. The kids tell you they don't like their dad. He's grumpy, rarely talks to them about their day, and acts more like a warden than a father.

OUTMANIPULATING THE MANIPULATOR:

Understanding Children's Manipulative Styles

J ust as there are several parenting styles to choose from, kids often fall into distinct manipulative modes of behavior. Kids can be manipulative pros, and outmanipulating the manipulator can be a trying task for any parent. The first step in dealing with this is to realize that even very young children can select their emotions and behaviors based on the reaction they wish to receive from an adult. Once you accept the notion of child manipulation, you can become a more effective disciplinarian and not fall prey as frequently to children's tactics.

No matter how consistent you try to be as a parent, some kids are always looking for loopholes in the rules. Others will behave only if the consequence affects them intensely, and still others will spite themselves just to prove who is the boss. These kids are manipulative pros and fall within several categories.

The If-Then Kid

Sandy just couldn't understand it: Almost every time she asked her kids to do something, they'd ignore her request. Thirteen-year-old Danny and fifteen-year-old Benjamin were good kids—rarely talked back, came in on time, and were reasonably polite in school. But Sandy had to yell or become angry before they acknowledged her, and then only begrudgingly would they pick up their dirty clothes or put their dishes in the sink. And the boys weren't much better for their father, Larry. They ignored his requests also, complying only when Dad really became angry and looked as if he might physically pick them up and drop them off in their bedrooms to clean up their mess. But neither Sandy nor Larry wanted to resort to physical means to control their kids. They just wanted them to do as told, when told.

A few years ago I had worked with the family who lived next door, and that mom suggested they come to see me. We had worked out similar problems with her two daughters, and Sandy was hopeful that the same techniques would be effective with her boys.

I met first with the parents, to get a history of the family dynamics—who was the main disciplinarian, what consequences were being used, and how the kids reacted to the consequences. I heard the typical answers—both parents felt they disciplined equally. Well, they did nag and yell at the boys at about the same rate and frequency, but I showed them that that really wasn't discipline—it was basically a waste of time. They learned that their children didn't react positively to their requests because the consequences meant very little to the boys. I noted that we would have to come up with more effective consequences if we were to get their attention.

Interviewing the guys was fun. They were conniving and manipulative, aware of how they maneuvered their parents, and honest in admitting that they knew what they were doing. I asked them what things and activities mattered to them the most. Danny mentioned CDs, money, and clothing, and Benjamin was focused on getting his driver's license and a car for his sixteenth birthday.

When I gave them the acid test—"Would you listen better to your folks if getting things that you wanted depended upon your behavior?"—both boys admitted that they probably would, but didn't think that their parents would follow through with it.

I then interviewed the entire family. I explained to Larry and

Sandy that they would probably have more success with the boys if they tied their requests to consequences such as material things as well as privileges.

Sandy felt uncomfortable with this. She thought that it would be bribing her kids just to do what they should be doing as a member of the family. My argument was that the boys were what I called *if-then* kids. This is the type of child who will respond appropriately only when the parent says something to the effect of *"If* you don't stop this behavior, *then* I will punish you." I explained that most kids need to know the consequences of their actions before they decide whether they will act out or act appropriately. Larry and Sandy accepted my theory and committed to devising a behavior management program that would work for their two if-then kids.

In my experience the if-then kid is perhaps the most common kind of manipulator. Misbehavior and noncompliance are characteristics of if-then kids, and many children fall within this category at some point in their lives.

Parents continually claim that this was not the way it was when they were growing up. There are various versions of the tale, but most proceed as follows: "When I was a kid I wouldn't have dared to talk back to my parents, or my father would have walloped me." Another rendition is, "I did what my mother asked me to do just because she was my mom, and I was expected to comply." No doubt there are many adults today who truly acted appropriately as children. However, there were many if-then children in their generation also.

Most of us were acquainted with if-then kids as we were growing up. These were the youngsters who continually broke rules and tried to push the limits as much as possible. If their parents or teachers were not successful at consistently applying consequences for unacceptable behaviors, these if-then children of long ago have most likely evolved into if-then adults today.

If-then adults still continue to need rules to keep their behavior appropriate. *"If* you have an affair, *then* I will leave you" is a typical statement of the wife of an if-then husband. This threat may or may not be successful, depending upon whether the if-then husband values the marital relationship. Another version is, *"If* you do not come to work on time, *then* I will fire you." Too many if-then employees lose their jobs because the threat of being without work is not important enough to them, or they are lacking in the self-control necessary to follow the rules given by the employer.

The parents of an if-then child need to depend less upon their perception of the way they acted toward their parents when they were children and to focus more upon the ways in which their own kids are behaving. To expect your child to be reasonable because "that's the way it should be" or "that's the way I was for my parents" may be unrealistic. Practical parenting involves perceiving your kids in a realistic manner and developing appropriate expectations for them.

If a parent is lucky enough to have a reasonable child, talking with the youngster will most likely be effective. But even the most reasonable of children will become if-then kids occasionally. However, if the frequency of acting out is low, occasional outbursts are generally tolerable.

It is the child who continually needs the if-then parental approach who wears down the parent. The adult must persevere, always responding with very clear rules. This is necessary if the parent is to continue to control the situation. When the parent becomes exhausted and gives in, the child will manipulate even more. In other words, the adult must learn to *outmanipulate the manipulator.*

• • •

The Guilt-Provoking Kid

Another type of manipulative child is the *guilt provoker*. Kids know their parents' "hot buttons," as in the case of fifteen-year-old Linda and her father, Ed. Linda was in trouble for inappropriate behavior at school. After Ed had finished lecturing her on why she should not talk back to her teachers, she erupted with "I see you yelling at Mom, and nothing happens to you!" This caught Ed off guard, and his wife, Donna, subtly agreed with Linda since this was something she had been trying to discuss with her husband for some time. The issue now turns to a marital conflict rather than a child behavior problem. Pretty smart kid, that Linda!

Or consider Andrew, who was beginning to skip school. This sixteen-year-old knew that his mother was very anxious about his shaky social relationships. He had noticed that his mother would become sympathetic to his plight if he was socially rejected or appeared to be depressed. He told her that he had skipped class because he felt picked on by a boy earlier in the day.

However, Andrew actually skipped because he had not completed his homework assignment the night before and did not wish to be given a detention. He had chosen the social rejection excuse because he knew that it would pull his mom off track. Andrew's thinking was, "If Mom does not see through this smoke screen, I may be able to convince her that is why I skipped class." If Mom goes along with this, Andrew will learn the inappropriate lesson that using lying and guilt to manipulate and provoke people may temporarily accomplish one's goals.

Guilt provoking is perhaps the most effective manipulatory technique that a school-age child can employ. The unsuspecting parent may find herself tangled in a web of feeling responsible for her child's actions and self-concept. This can be paralyzing because the parent fears that any negative action taken may push the child into one of her moods again. However, appropriate consequences can defuse the situation if the parent is perceptive and realizes that he or she is being had.

The best way to determine whether your child is pulling your strings or really feels bad about a situation is to look for an emerging pattern. For instance, if your daughter talks about being lonely only when you have reprimanded her, most likely she's using the "poor me" routine as a red herring to gain your sympathy and to get you off her back for the original crime she committed. However, if she appears depressed without any apparent pattern or reason, you should talk seriously with her about her moods and consider getting her professional help.

There are three other types of children who are capable of driving their parents crazy and who will benefit from more structure in their lives. The first two, the child with a *wandering conscience* and the *pit-Mom-against-Dad* kid, both tend to be experts at manipulation. The third category, the *chameleon kid,* displays behavioral problems more as a reaction to fuzzy or nonexistent parental rules than as a maneuver to control the situation. Let's take a look at each of these kids, starting with the latter.

The Chameleon Kid

Chameleon kids are children who respond to the rules of whatever environment they find themselves in. When given adequate rules and structure, they will generally comply well, and some people may swear that they are angelic. But in a situation without rules and consistent guidelines, these kids may become noncompliant and disruptive.

Eleven-year-old Raymond is such a preadolescent. He's in the sixth grade and deals with six teachers each day as he moves from subject to subject. Four of the teachers find him delightful, but two, his Spanish and physical fitness teachers, are pulling out their hair.

At a school conference I attended with Raymond, his guidance counselor, parents, and teachers, it sounded as if we were talking about two different kids—Raymond and his evil twin. The four who were experiencing little or no difficulty explained that they wrote homework assignments and test/quiz dates on the board each day and that they consistently checked to see whether the students turned in their work and were prepared for exams. Classwork and homework were collected daily, and review sessions for tests were part of the curriculum. The students knew exactly what was expected of them and were clearly informed as to how many points each assignment or test was worth. In addition, inappropriate behaviors such as talking while the teacher was lecturing, leaving one's seat, and rudeness led immediately to lost grade points as well as to a detention. One teacher was even available for "Saturday school"—a four-hour weekend detention given after three infractions were earned in a grading period.

These four teachers all had one thing in common. They set clear guidelines as to what was expected of the students in terms of both work performance and behavior and gave out appropriate consequences depending upon the students' actions. Raymond and his classmates respected (and perhaps slightly feared) the teachers and complied well with the system.

However, the Spanish and physical fitness teachers took a laissez-faire approach. In Spanish, homework was assigned but only intermittently collected, so that Raymond tended to roll the dice and not complete his work. The teacher was wary of angering the kids by handing out detentions, and the kids picked up on this lax attitude and began to abuse the situation. The teacher did more whining than teaching, and the classroom soon became chaotic. Raymond, being a chameleon kid, slipped into this mode easily and became disruptive himself.

His physical fitness class was similar. The kids could choose to work out or not, feigning a pulled muscle in order to avoid lifting weights or spending the period horsing around at the back of the gym. Not only did these kids learn little from the curriculum, they were disruptive and frequently were sent to the assistant principal for reprimand.

The Chameleon Kid

Alexis's Mom

When it came time for Alexis to begin high school, she begged to attend the local public school, which is very large and known for its rebellious kids. After many debates I agreed to a trial period—reluctantly, because she had attended a small private school up to that point. Within a few weeks her personality began to change. The way she spoke or didn't speak was sending me clear messages. I was the "enemy." She would answer me in one-word sentences or choose to ignore me if she didn't like the topic. Her grades went from B's in middle school to D's and F's in high school, and she no longer talked to her friends from her old private school. She now had friends who were party-planning, school-skipping underachievers with no care or plans for their future. Her dress also changed dramatically. Alexis now wore oversized everything—T-shirts, jeans, jackets, sweatshirts, and sneakers. After two years of broken promises and a failed grade level, Dr. Peters arranged for Alexis to return to a small private school. Within a few months she made new friends, started wearing clothes that actually fit her, held conversations with us, came home before curfew, and pulled up her grades. Now she will even graduate on time. Our relationship is where it should be. My daughter is a pleasure to be around and we go on shopping trips, out to lunch, and to the movies. I have my daughter back again.

Alexis

I can see clearly now that I was an unbearable child when I was at public high school. I was arrogant and foolish. I wanted to do what I wanted when I wanted, without having curfews or guidance—especially from my mom. I despised my mom, and I even ran away.

> *Now that I am older and have looked back on my actions I realize what I was like. I now go to private school and I don't have an attitude. I don't talk back, obey my curfew, and get along with my mom. We have built up our relationship again, and we can go out together without arguing the whole time. She listens to me, and I listen to her.*

At the school conference the parents and teachers realized that Raymond was basically a good kid, but one who responded to the structure—or lack of it—in his environment. Mom noted that he listened much better to her than to his father. She explained that she controlled the purse strings, and that if Raymond didn't do his daily chores or was rude to her, he would lose part of his weekly allowance. His father usually just "spoke with the boy" and tried reasoning with him when he was rude. He would listen politely to his dad, but the rude behavior would continue to occur because Dad's rules were ambiguous and the consequences were weak. Raymond is a good kid—there is no "evil Raymond," just the chameleon changing his color (behavior) depending upon the twig (situation) he finds himself in.

If yours is a chameleon kid, be prepared to set up significant structure in his life. This may take the form of weeding out friends who are not good influences, choosing teachers who are structured, and setting up a clear and comprehensive daily schedule of what you expect each day from your child. Chameleon kids tend to need black-and-white situations; ambiguity or shades of gray allow the child to slip through loopholes. Try to predict "cracks" in the child's schedule and expectations, and fill them so that he can't fall through.

The Wandering-Conscience Kid

The *wandering-conscience* kid is tougher to handle. I believe that one's conscience or superego is based upon both genetic and environmental factors. This is an example of the nature-nurture argument that pervades much of psychological thought.

Psychologists have studied the conscience for decades, and generally conclude that people seem to be born with a baseline level—a mental zone within which one makes choices about what is right and what is wrong and how to act upon these choices. Some kids appear to be born with a rigid set of rules, whereas others impulsively decide how to act. Their decisions seem to depend upon a variety of issues including what's in it for them, how tolerant they are feeling at the moment, and whether they are bored or not.

The environment that these wandering-conscience kids are raised in can play a very important role in contributing to the quality and breadth of conscience. If these children are left to their own devices, the zone is usually quite wide, allowing them to rationalize harmful behavior to others. Many just don't care about the effect that their actions have upon other people.

However, if raised in a home with clear, concise, and consistent rules, wandering-conscience kids can be taught the limits of the zone. They may try to push the boundaries, but most often they will behave because they are aware of the negative consequences they will receive if the rules are broken.

I believe that many of the children we see in juvenile justice programs are wandering-conscience kids. These youngsters might have been saved from the system if their parents had taken the time and displayed the guts to make and follow through with rules. Even children in families in which criminal behavior flourishes can be taught to keep their behavior within an acceptable zone, but only if there is a caring adult who is willing to devote himself to this endeavor. Too often, parents expect others—teachers, ministers, judges—to "talk sense" into their children. There must be an adult in the life of the wandering-conscience child who closely supervises and guides her, working daily to keep her on track. If the child's parents have a wandering conscience themselves, this guidance will most likely not occur. However, one parent or an involved relative or friend can do the job.

I've found that one of the best therapies for the wandering-conscience kid is to arrange a visit to the local juvenile court where he can observe firsthand what fate befalls those who choose not to abide by society's rules. A trip to the police station or even a conference with the child's school resource officer can also be enlightening. Although such a field trip will not instantaneously change the wandering-conscience kid's personality, it will give him pause to think—and I've seen many kids reconsider their behavior as a result of such a visit.

Wandering-conscience kids need to be presented early on with the blueprint of what differentiates right from wrong. They may not internally feel the difference, but after a while they may begin to act upon it, to be less impulsive and to make better choices. This "fake it until you make it" behavior may work. It means changing the external behavior first in the hope that changes in the child's internal attitude (his conscience) will follow. If true attitudinal changes do not occur, such as the child's sincerely empathizing with others and accepting the need for rules, at least he's practicing appropriate behavior and realizing that this will keep him out of trouble.

Brad is a good example of a child with a wandering conscience. He was fourteen when I first met him, brought to my office by his desperate and somewhat embarrassed parents. Brad was definitely the black sheep of the family. His three sisters were stars at school and at home, but since moving to our area a year before, Brad had begun to get into trouble.

He had always been a handful—a real risk taker, the first in his group to try smoking cigarettes and skipping school. But in his old hometown he had been placed in a small private school where all of his teachers knew exactly what was happening with Brad on a day-to-day basis, and they could nip problems in the bud. Communication between home and school was easy, and Brad found it difficult to get away with much before his parents would find out.

However, when the mother was transferred to a new job and the family relocated to my area, they chose to enroll all of the kids in rather large public schools. Brad loved this—he could slip through the cracks with ease. His teachers were too busy to contact the parents when he misbehaved or skipped school.

By the time I met him, he had accumulated quite a laundry list of infractions ranging from petty theft to breaking and entering. His parents installed a home burglar system in order to *keep Brad in,* set up so that it would go off as he tried to sneak out of his window at night. But this guy was no amateur—he soon learned how to tape a magnet to the sensor mechanism on his bedroom window, which short-circuited the system as he slipped out.

Brad impressed me with his intelligence and craftiness. He seemed to be constantly thinking of ways to get around doing things rather than just getting them done correctly the first time. It was like a game to him—scoring points when he thwarted authority, bragging to his friends that he was above the rules.

But in his own way Brad was a nice kid. He never set out to hurt anyone, but people around him tended to get into trouble just by associating with him. At times he would leave my office with what seemed like the very best of intentions, only to follow his nose and do whatever made him feel best later that day. He often expressed remorse to me for his actions, but I doubted that he was really sincere. Brad knew he was supposed to feel bad after taking his father's car and damaging the fender, but I felt that his true emotion was anger that he had been caught.

After a few months of therapy I could tell that Brad was not going to profit from my work with him. He had too much freedom in his life—skipping school, sneaking out at night. Therefore, it was difficult for his parents to give him consequences that they could stick with. Since both folks worked, Brad came and went, often coming home well into the evening even on school nights.

I arranged for him to attend a residential military school in a neighboring state. Brad was not pleased when I initially discussed this idea with him, but he warmed up to it as he realized he would be living in a dormitory with guys his age and that his parents would not be there to hassle him. Little did he realize that military schools have tight restrictions (early curfews, mandatory study hall) and consequences that had some teeth to them (demerits, loss of weekend passes, and marching in "the yard").

I heard that he pushed the limits the first three weeks he was there, but after having to march the yard on a regular basis, Brad apparently realized that he no longer could work around the system. The commandant didn't cave in to his pleas for forgiveness and treated Brad just like the rest of the cadets—privileges and rank promotions for appropriate behavior, loss of freedoms and marching in circles for inappropriate actions.

By his third month at school, Brad had begrudgingly learned to work within the system. He still sometimes acted impulsively and continued to put in some time marching the yard, but he was able to keep his behavior within bounds so that he earned several weekend passes home.

He visited me during his second semester, all decked out in his dress blues. Brad actually appeared somewhat proud of himself for making it work within the system, and the uniform sure looked great on him! His parents had adjusted to the realization that their son would most likely need to finish his high school career at military school, since they could not provide the supervision and structure that he needed when he lived at home.

The Wandering-Conscience Kid

Rebecca's Stepmom

Two years ago I married the man of my dreams and became step-mother to a ten-year-old girl named Rebecca who was diagnosed with attention deficit disorder, with an emphasis on impulsivity.* Those words cannot begin to express the emotional trauma such a child can bring daily into one's home. When my fiancé proposed, his daughter was so excited she immediately asked if she could call me Mom even though her mother is living. I was surprised, but I agreed to it and in fact asked her to be my maid of honor. That camaraderie lasted the first week. I soon realized that her sweetness was not genuine, but in fact a manipulation game.

No matter what Rebecca was instructed to do, she would do what she pleased and then lie about her actions. For example, she systematically used her bike handle to scratch my new car. I was puzzled by the damage as I watched it grow day by day. My grown son and I walked into the garage one day and caught her in the act, but she said, "I didn't make all those marks! I didn't even know it was happening!" Rebecca also set fire to a roll of toilet paper in her room, physically hurt her preschool cousin, and wrote a letter to her father that said she hated him and wanted him dead for punishing her. She has no conscience; in her mind, she is not responsible for her own actions. She is now on Dr. Peters' behavior management program for the second time. The first time I was in charge, and it did not work—her mean streaks were too much for me, and being the stepmom, I gave up. Currently her father is in charge of the schedule and is consistent in his discipline with her. We are hopeful that it is working, but time will tell. Only our faith and our love for each other has kept our marriage together.

*See Chapter 8 for a discussion of attention deficit disorder.

Brad is an extreme case, but there are lots of Brads in this world. These wandering-conscience kids do not set out to hurt anyone, but end up doing so in their impulsive quest for a good time. Brad's behavior was under control when he was at a private school—he was younger and less mobile. But the freedom of attending a large public high school with friends who drove was just too much for him to handle. He couldn't deal with the everyday responsibilities that many kids adjust to naturally, and only a regimented situation such as is found in a military school provided the supervision that Brad needed.

Incidentally, I heard from Brad a few months ago. He's now in the Navy and engaged to a girl he met while away at school. Brad is still Brad, but I picked up from our phone conservation that he now acknowledges his impulsivity, and although he continues to have thoughts of acting inappropriately, he's learned that the consequences are just not worth it. I feel good for Brad, but I have a sneaky suspicion that I'll be seeing Bradley, Jr., in my office someday!

The Pit-Mom-Against-Dad Kid

Finally, we have the *pit-Mom-against-Dad* variety of manipulative child. These guys are especially tricky—you often have to be on your toes to keep up with them. The parent who consistently responds to a child's request with "ask your mother/father" is a sitting duck. The child sees the opening, zooms in with something like "Mom, Dad said to check with you if I can go to the mall. He didn't seem to have a problem with it." The child's hope is that Mom, especially if she is busy, will go along with the idea thinking that her husband has already discussed the pros and cons and is in agreement with the child.

But, lo and behold, as soon as the parents hear the front door slam they begin to go over the "five W's"—the who, what, where, when, and why of the excursion—and neither has a clue what their kid is up to. And whom do they usually get mad at? Yep, that's right—each other! And as they are arguing and accusing, the kid is merrily on his way to who knows where, with whomever, to do who knows what.

I describe this type of manipulative child as "squirrely" because they are so good at setting up a situation and finding loopholes to scamper through. Parents of squirrely kids need to develop an effective communication system. Children should be told, "I want to know the five W's of your request, and if you can't or refuse to give me the information or if I feel uncomfortable with your answers, then you just can't go."

Make sure that the other spouse has signed off on the idea also. I have some of my trickier clients get permission in writing from both parents, including a description of the five W's. The paper is stuck to the refrigerator door with a magnet so that there is no question whether the child is acting in compliance with his parents' wishes or whether he has ignored them.

Sheila is probably the most proficient "pit-Mom-against-Dad" kid that I have seen in a long time. She's risen to this status by virtue of her parents' work schedules. Dad has the 7:00 A.M. to 3:00 P.M. shift at the local power plant and Mom works 3:00 P.M. to 11:00 P.M. at the hospital. Sheila couldn't have planned it better if she had set up the schedules herself! She arrives home from middle school at around 2:40 P.M., just in time for her mother to ask how school went and to run out the door.

At least twice a week Sheila requests permission from her mother to go somewhere, usually her friend's house or to ride her bike to the local convenience store. More often than not, Mom's mind is set on getting to work on time and she tells Sheila to ask her dad when he gets home.

So what would any red-blooded pit-Mom-against-Dad kid do in this situation? Well, he or she would leave, and so does Sheila. When Dad comes home to an empty house, he panics and calls his wife, who has just started her nursing shift and is overwhelmed with her responsibilities. She informs him that she told Sheila to ask him before leaving and questions why he is bothering her at work when he's the one who is supposed to be dealing with Sheila at that time.

This would happen over and over again. When Sheila returned from her outing, she would have an endless array of excuses for her father. "Mom didn't say no," or "I told Mom where I wanted to go," or "I knew you wouldn't mind because you've let me go to Jenny's plenty of times before."

Well, needless to say, Sheila's folks ended up with many arguments and some hefty marital problems, and began seeing one of my associates for marital therapy. While she worked on their anger and disagreements, I focused on solving what came to be known as the "Sheila problem." It was soon apparent that this was a communication and rule-setting issue that we could deal with easily.

In therapy we set up the following rules and communication tactics:

- Sheila was to come home directly from the school bus. If Mom didn't see her by 2:45, she was to drive to the bus stop and determine why Sheila was late.

- Sheila was not allowed to ask her mother's permission to do anything while on "Dad's shift." She had to stay in the house and wait until he got home to ask his permission.

- If Dad said yes, then yes it was. Since Mom was not at home to discuss the situation nor able to take extensive phone calls at work, she would have to trust Dad's judgment and back up his decisions.

- Because there was often at least forty-five minutes between Mom leaving for work and Dad arriving home, Mom was to call Sheila on her car phone on her way to work, or from the hospital after she arrived. If Sheila did not immediately answer the telephone, Mom would call back in about five minutes, allowing for the possibility of a bathroom break. Since the family had call waiting, the line should never be busy, and therefore Sheila could not take the phone off the hook and leave for a while, later saying that she was talking with one of her friends and that's why Mom couldn't reach her.

We set up consequences for breaking these rules and wrote up an agreement, and all three family members signed it. Sheila was a bit miffed that she no longer could wiggle out of situations, but her parents had significantly fewer arguments, and they soon were able to terminate marital therapy successfully. All it took was a communication setup that was convenient and fail proof to keep this pit-Mom-against-Dad kid under control!

All of these manipulative kids are trying, at the least—and downright awful in some cases—but whether your child is an if-then kid, guilt provoker, chameleon kid, one with a wandering conscience, or a pit-Mom-against-Dad professional, the solution tends to be the same. You need to set up clear guidelines and consequences and to stick to the program. You are, after all, quite capable of taking control, but you may have not realized how to use the creative parenting power you possess.

Keeping or taking back control of your kid is a lot easier than living with a manipulative child. It may be tough at first to turn the tables on him, but once you have his attention and he realizes that you will do something (not just lecture or nag or try to reason) you'll see much greater cooperation and compliance, and significantly less manipulation.

THE BENEVOLENT DICTATOR:

The Parenting Style That Works

The manipulative kids discussed in the last chapter all have one characteristic in common—in different ways they are all trying to run the show, often without taking into account the effect their behaviors have upon others. In my practice I have found that parenting as a *benevolent dictator* (kindly letting your children know that they have a vote, but that you are the final decision maker), rather than parenting as a "democracy" (often a free-for-all), to be the most effective manner of teaching children frustration tolerance and self-control. The parent has greater control and establishes more stability in the home. In his book *Parent Power!: A Common-Sense Approach to Parenting in the '90s and Beyond,* John Rosemond suggests that benevolent dictators do not "demand unquestioning obedience. They encourage questions, but make the final decisions. They restrict their children's freedom, but they are not tyrants. They restrict in order to protect and guide. . . . Life with a Benevolent Dictator is predictable and secure for children." In choosing a benevolent dictatorship the parent understands that although he may feel guilty and perhaps sorry for the child when he has to be punished, the kid will profit from receiving the consequence rather than being taught the wrong lesson—that misbehavior will be tolerated.

Kids learn self-control when parents create boundaries and set limits for their children. The old adage "It was almost as if he was asking to be punished" is quite apt. One often sees children who appear to be more content after limits have been set for them. Children usually do not ask for limit setting, but their temperaments tend to improve when they know what they can get away with and what they can't.

For example, ten-year-old Marcia constantly begged her parents to allow her to stay up later at night. Her parents felt that 9:00 P.M. was an appropriate bedtime, but Marcia often didn't get to bed until after 9:30 P.M. After attending counseling and learning about limit setting, her parents were able to set more strict guidelines. Marcia was in bed by 9:00 P.M., and following two weeks of a firm commitment to this bedtime by her parents, she actually slept better, awoke with a good attitude, and was a more reasonable child since she was receiving more rest each night. Marcia was a happier child because her parents were willing to risk conflict with her in order to do what was best.

Do all folks need to parent as a benevolent dictator? It depends. Some lucky parents have easy children (babies who sleep through the night, toddlers who add "okay" and "yes" to their vocabularies, grade schoolers who do their homework without too many parental threats, middle schoolers who believe that trying drugs is a stupid idea, high schoolers who still talk to their parents and perhaps even listen to them once in a while, and adult children who leave home without having to be kicked out). These types of kids I like to call *keepers.* They probably can be raised in a more democratic household because they naturally tend not to abuse others or to take advantage of situations. You may know a family blessed with a youngster who appears by nature to be reasonable. But although these easygoing, self-motivated youngsters do exist, they appear to be the exception rather than the rule.

In his book *The Nature of the Child,* psychologist Jerome Kagan cites many studies showing that temperament is largely inborn.

For example, babies who are born with a tendency toward extreme timidity tend to remain shy and inhibited as they mature. This does not mean that once the child's "blueprint" has been ascertained the parent should meekly accept it—"My child was ornery from the beginning, and therefore this is a lost cause." In fact, quite the opposite is true.

Environmental influence plays a very important part in molding personality and behavior. Easy children may need less molding—just a firm look from the parent may do the trick. Difficult children may need more guidance, such as time-outs or having privileges removed. The trick is to determine as early as possible which type of child you are raising and to use this information to develop your own disciplinary plan.

Even the most compliant child often reaches a testy stage when she digs her heels in and demands unreasonable privileges. You'll realize that this has occurred when you feel yourself in conflict with your child even after you've tried to be reasonable and to explain your decision thoroughly, and she still sees it only from her perspective. Some kids reach this stage later than others, but most will eventually evidence some rebellious behavior. Parents need to be able to recognize the testy stage as a normal phase of development and to deal with it effectively.

So whether your child is an easygoing, compliant kid or one who makes his living giving you gray hair, it's necessary to develop a behavioral plan. Consistent, effective discipline given in a nonchalant manner is the trick. Just the thought of this may sound overwhelming. Parents with overcontrolling, unselfdisciplined children find it difficult to imagine that they can even come close to achieving this goal.

Dealing with the inappropriate behavior of elementary-age children, preteens, and teenagers is often more complex than what is necessary for younger children. From age seven on, kids are capable of understanding perfectly well what their limits are if their parents set boundaries for them. Limits should follow the *four C's.* They must be *concise, clear, consistent,* and—at times—*catastrophic.*

Concise and clear limits are mandatory in terms of rule setting because children have a way of finding loopholes. The youngster who has been told not to overfeed the fish in the morning may feed the fish too much in the evening. His indignant retort to the parent who wishes to punish the child may be "You told me not to overfeed the fish in the morning, but you didn't say anything about overfeeding them in the evening!" Parents can easily become exasperated by this type of manipulation and should establish rules in broad and encompassing terms such as, *"Never overfeed the fish!"*

Children are human computers when keeping mental track of parental inconsistencies, so consequences for inappropriate behaviors should be applied consistently. For example, the child may say, "You didn't punish me yesterday for bugging my brother, so it's unfair to send me to my room today." The child does have a point. The parent is sending mixed messages, and the child will use this to his advantage.

Dr. Fitzhugh Dodson suggests in his book *How to Discipline with Love: From Crib to College* that successful parents believe how they parent directly affects how their children behave, and accordingly they take care to discipline their kids consistently. Secondly, they are not afraid to confront their children, even if this means a temporary rift between the parent and child. The parents' ability to put negative emotions from the child ("I hate you for sending me to my room!") into proper perspective is essential. Consistent discipline (the teaching of rules and consequences for maintaining or breaking rules) appears to be the key element.

The last C involves catastrophic consequences. I'm not advocating corporal punishment. Personally, I believe that kids respond better to other negative consequences, such as time-out, but I have met families in my practice who swear that a pop on the butt (or even just the threat of it) works wonders. There are many other consequences you can use that will get your kid's attention and lead to considerably better behavior, but the consequences have to be *important* to the child in order to have an effect.

BEHAVIOR MANAGEMENT GROUND RULES

Most families with noncompliant children have literally tried everything before seeking professional advice. Disciplinary tactics that they have employed often include spanking, time-out, removing privileges, and—most notable—lecturing.

Parents often tell me that each of these consequences seems to work for a short time, but the effectiveness soon dissipates. Generally they give in and stop the punishment due to their own guilt or exhaustion. Parents come to the counselor's office at wit's end, looking for a magic cure. But they find that magic does not exist. The solution involves common sense and lots of effort but is quite workable if they are willing to take some chances, stand up to their kids, and learn the basics of managing their children's behavior. What follows is a discussion of the basic ground rules parents need to use in order for a behavior management program to work.

Consistency

First, let's explore consistency. Most parents try to follow through with what rules they do establish, but many succumb to the sabotaging techniques of their kids.

Youngsters are professionals at wearing parents down, and why shouldn't they be? They have more energy and fewer responsibilities than adults, and can be very persistent in order to get their way. Sixteen-year-old Tom continued to bug his mother, Sue, about taking the car and going to activities in the next county. Sue felt uncomfortable because he was a new driver, and tried to talk him into going places closer to home. But Tom was determined, because he had already told his girlfriend that he was going to pick her up that evening. Tom came up with every reason, excuse, and idea he could think of to talk his mother into it. After three grueling hours, Sue finally caved in and gave permission. It just wasn't worth it to fight with him anymore. Chalk one up for Tom!

However, if Sue had been able to stand her ground with her son, he would have had to comply or else face losing his car privileges totally. After all, his mother held the keys not only to the car, but also to her son's behavior—if only she had the stamina to outlast his nagging campaign.

Nine-year-old Nicholas was also a pro at deciphering his mother's moods and going in for the kill exactly at the right moment. Although on restriction for lying, he continually asked his mom if he could go outside to play. Every time he asked, she said "no," which was followed by Nicholas's "why not?" At first Mom would explain to him why he couldn't go out, and after a while she began to ignore him. But nothing seemed to stop Nicholas's nagging. Finally, as she was having difficulty getting the baby down for her nap, Mom relented and let Nicholas leave—just so she could have some peace and quiet and perhaps get the baby to settle down.

When I asked Nicholas if this was true, this brilliant strategist described his tactic to me. "After asking Mom five or six times to go out she usually either yells at me and sends me to my room or lets me go outside. Going to my room is no big deal. I read my comic books. So I've really got nothing to lose if I bug her, and sometimes it works!"

When Mom heard his reasoning, she was furious with Nicholas.

She should, however, have been mad at herself, since she was the one who was caving in. She was actually *teaching* her son to be manipulative due to her inconsistency.

Also, be careful about threatening consequences that you cannot follow through with. Don't threaten to remove your daughter's bike for a year, because you probably won't. A week is easy to do and still stings a bit. To remain consistent you may have to soften the consequence in order to guarantee that you'll really follow through with it.

Effective Consequences

Disciplinary tactics that are effective for one family may not work well for another. The effectiveness of any consequence varies depending upon factors such as the number of kids in the family, the children's ages, and the home environment.

In determining if a consequence will work for you, ask yourself, "Will *this* consequence make an impression on *this* child?" If it is a reward, is it appealing to the particular youngster? Meghan may love new clothes, whereas Laurie couldn't care less about them. Television, telephone, and music may be rewarding to some teens, while others treasure freedom and the use of the car.

Negative consequences also must make an impression. The issue regarding punishments should be, "Will *this* punishment be meaningful to *this* child and bother him enough so that the inappropriate behavior decreases?" Fifteen minutes of time-out normally will not affect an eleven-year-old, but one hour should, and if it doesn't, ninety minutes spent in time-out may make the kid think twice!

Tailoring the consequences to the individual child is mandatory. A teenager who practically lives on the telephone will change almost any inappropriate behavior if telephone privileges are threatened to be removed, while an introverted youngster may respond more to taking away her favorite books or hobbies. The eight-year-old boy who is obsessed with cartoons, the fifteen-year-old girl addicted to clothes, and the eleven-year-old miser saving up quarters for a new toy will all respond if these particular motivators are used.

Negative Consequences

Taking Away

Families have many types of negative consequences available to them. Loss of possessions, attention, and privileges are common. For instance, permanently taking a CD or two or removing the TV from your adolescent's bedroom most likely will get her attention, and she'll begin to believe that you mean business in the future. Most parents, however, do not take away enough or make the loss significant—losing TV time for an hour can easily be tolerated by a twelve-year-old, but loss of all "electricity" (TV, Nintendo, and telephone) for an entire day really has an impact! Too often, however, we continue to use inconsequential punishments over and over again, without being creative or imposing other possibly more effective measures.

Time-out

Time-out is both a physical and a psychological condition. Physically, a time-out setting is a safe place where the child must go for a specified period of time. Psychologically, time-out is the placement of the child away from all attention and interesting activities. This allows the kid to consider what rule she has broken in order to have been placed in time-out, as well as to think about how to avoid being put there again in the near future.

Setting

The optimal time-out situation is an empty bedroom, but most rooms will suffice if they are emptied of interesting or potentially dangerous objects. One must be concerned with scissors, medications, etc., and remove these from the room since the child, when placed in time-out, may be quite angry and inadvertently harm himself. Place the child in the time-out room for a set period of time. The amount of time varies according to the age and personality of the child. Parents often hear from their pediatricians that they should allow one minute of time-out for each year of the child's age. In my experience, eight minutes for an eight-year-old probably won't make a dent. You may find that doubling that amount of time will get your kid's attention. The seven-year-old may need fifteen minutes, whereas the twelve-year-old usually needs at least half an hour of time-out for his misdeed to sink in. Especially ornery adolescents may require a few hours of time-out in order to gain their attention.

Keeping the Child in Time-out

Some kids need to have the door closed during time-out since they tend to leave the room. If the child opens the door and leaves the room, then the door may need to be locked from the outside. This will eliminate the need for parents to become physically involved in putting the child back in time-out.

I suggest that you give little or no attention to your kid during time-out. Youngsters need to learn that their parents are in control and will resort to placing them in a boring, safe situation when they lose self-control or become overly demanding. If an empty bedroom is not available, a safe bathroom or the child's own bedroom may suffice.

It is important to remember that the purpose of time-out is to gain the child's attention, not to place him in a harmful environment. Whenever the time-out situation is employed, it must be safe, boring, well lit, and well ventilated. Time-out is effective because it bores the child, not because it harms him.

Use of the Timer

The use of a kitchen timer is very helpful when employing time-out as a negative consequence. The timer is placed outside of the room and is set for the allotted period. The child knows that time-out is over when the buzzer rings and that the parent will remove him from the situation only at that time. This eliminates the need for you to constantly respond to the child's persistent questions: "Is it time yet?" "When can I come out?"

When the buzzer rings, the time-out is over. The less you communicate with your kid during time-out, the better. If your kid perceives that he has you upset, he may feel that he has won the conflict. In reality, no one wins in control disputes. These situations should be looked upon as learning experiences, not as notches on a gun barrel by either the parent or the youngster. You'll soon experience that time-out is a very powerful technique that will help you regain your composure and emphasize to the child that you truly are in control.

Positive Consequences

In terms of rewarding kids, parents have several effective options. Activity, social, and material rewards are the most common reinforcers.

Activity Rewards

Activity or privilege rewards can be quite effective with kids. Children in elementary school enjoy playing board games, going for a bike ride, or taking a trip to the mall. Preteens and teenagers like playing video games, spending private time with their friends, watching TV, and talking on the telephone. Again, be sure that the activity you choose is one that your child enjoys and values.

Social Rewards

Social rewards are parental behaviors such as praise and attention. Kids crave their parents' approval and will work to receive it. Teenagers prefer being praised for a job well done, whereas elementary school-age kids often secretly enjoy a hug or a good-natured "noogie" to the head.

Material Rewards

The third major type of reward involves giving material objects. Most kids will work for material rewards such as clothing and money. Often I suggest using poker chips in lieu of cash—they are easier to use and keep track of. Instead of a weekly allowance given without strings attached, a daily "cash" poker chip can be earned if the child has displayed appropriate behavior. If using clothing as a reward, the parent determines approximately how much money is spent for the child's clothing over one month, six months, or one year. The parent then decides how much this would equal on a daily basis. For example, if the parent spends approximately seven hundred dollars per year on clothing for her daughter, then the poker chip earned daily may be worth approximately two dollars. The child can then earn one clothing poker chip per day as part of a behavior management system. This amount is to be spent on clothing only. The parents may decide that they will provide some necessities such as socks, underwear, winter coats, and reasonably priced shoes, and have the child budget his clothing chips for all other clothing purchases.

One of the outcomes of this technique is that children learn to spend money wisely. Initially, many kids tend to be extravagant and to buy expensive designer clothing. However, when the child realizes that the parent is not going to be buying any clothing except for essentials, she usually begins to look for sales and will become more prudent in spending her own money.

I caution parents not to interfere with the child's selections. She has to learn how to handle spending money herself, even if mistakes are made at the beginning of the clothing poker chip system. If you let her make her own decisions, she'll learn to take responsibility for mistakes and not blame errors of judgment on you.

Parental Nonchalance

Parents need to practice the fine art of parental nonchalance. Saying calmly, "If you don't stop tantrumming, I'll take away your favorite toy," and walking away is a good example. If the child continues to throw a fit, take away the toy as you said you would.

If you aren't nonchalant, you'll be sure prey for your youngster, because kids love to push their parents' hot buttons. What could more controlling (and amusing) than merely talking back to an adult and seeing the parent's face flush, arms move frantically, and teeth clench? Some children delight in the control they gain when they can cause so many physiological changes in an adult! It's almost worth the punishment. The nonchalant parent, though, informs the youngster of the transgression and the consequence and then enforces the punishment, quickly and without flinching. Score one for Mom!

Sound easy? Not necessarily. It may take weeks of practice, but the payoffs are enormous. Children will no longer feel they earn points for getting their parents angry; they will only receive negative consequences.

I've found that couples often seem to have an easier time achieving nonchalance than do single parents. When they feel that they are becoming unglued, one parent can hand the situation over to the other, take a break, and reenter after having gained his or her composure. Single parents have to figure out a way to take a time-out for themselves if they feel that they are losing their composure, and come back to the situation after they have cooled down. Whether you are a single parent or have a partner, concurrent use of consistent, effective discipline given in a nonchalant manner allows you to gain (or to regain) control, and the family will become a more organized, pleasant unit.

Rule Setting

Before we proceed to the specific behavior management system in Chapter 6, a presentation of general rule-setting techniques is in order. When disciplining kids be sure to:

- Consistently reward good behavior and do so immediately.
- Punish inappropriate behavior with use of an effective negative consequence.
- Be careful not to reward inappropriate behavior.
- Follow Grandma's rule—"First work, then play."

Let's look at each of these. Rewarding good behavior and punishing inappropriate behavior are very important. For example, the parent who has been struggling with his kid to complete his homework without a hassle is all too typical. One evening, though, the youngster remains at the desk and finishes his math without complaining. Instead of ignoring this success, the parent chooses to note it by praising the child immediately. The child feels good and so does his father! However, had the child continued to complain and procrastinate, his father should have given him a negative consequence (such as no TV that night) because his son had previously been warned that homework complaints would no longer be tolerated.

The third point is that the parent who gives in to her child's constant hassling and complaining actually rewards the undesirable behavior. Kids have a tremendous ability to persevere. They can hassle a parent endlessly, especially if in the past the parent has given in to the child's demands. Be sure that your kids' whining never results in their getting what they want. Then they will learn to rephrase their complaints into appropriate requests.

The fourth point and a very important principle in rule setting is that behavior that leads to rewards will continue and behavior that does not will cease. This principle is commonly referred to as *Grandma's rule,* most likely because our foremothers were pretty smart cookies and employed it liberally. Grandma's rule states, "After you do your work, then you will get to play," or in practice, "After you clean up your room, then you can watch television or go outside."

All too often, though, parents tend to reverse Grandma's rule in terms of negotiating with their kids. For instance, the child may promise that he will clean up his room if only he can play a video game first. As many parents find out, the odds of the child cleaning up his room *after* he has played the video game are slim. Then the parent must reason with an unmotivated child (since he has already received his reward), and Dad finds himself again having been manipulated by the youngster. In this case, the child has sabotaged Grandma's rule and has actually been rewarded for his procrastination.

Now that the ground rules have been discussed, it's time to set up a behavior management system for your own home.

THE BEHAVIOR MANAGEMENT PROGRAM

I know, I know, many of you have tried star charts, smiley faces, and all kinds of gimmicks to motivate your kids to do their chores and to behave better. These programs all seem to work initially—the honeymoon effect. But when the novelty wears off, you're back to square one—threatening, nagging, and usually giving up. Kids are pros at figuring out how to get you off track, making you forget what you asked them to do, and causing you to be inconsistent regarding consequences. Okay, now that we've established that our kids are smart and sometimes sneaky, let's learn how to *outmanipulate the manipulator* by using behavior management.

When I describe the behavior management program to parents, one question that usually crops up is: "Doesn't this just scratch the surface and change my kid's behavior temporarily? What about the attitude causing the inappropriate behavior?" It's a good question, necessitating a somewhat complex answer.

To answer that question I need to talk a bit about the difference between behavioral and analytical psychologists. Behaviorists (that's me) are of the school of thought that changing the environment in some way—mainly through the use of positive and negative consequences—changes behavior. The change can be temporary if the consequence is weak or given infrequently, or can be permanent if the consequence is meaningful and given consistently. Behaviorists also believe that if a person changes a behavior for a long enough period of time, then the behavioral change actually leads to a change in attitude. For example, if a child is rewarded intensely and frequently for completing his homework, this behavior will improve dramatically. Successful homework leads to good grades, which in turn leads to positive academic self-esteem. Voila!—a true attitudinal change.

On the other hand, there are some schools of analytical psychology that propose that only long-term, in-depth analysis of feelings and life incidents leads to true attitudinal changes (these are the "talk therapy" folks). These psychologists feel that focusing upon earlier events and analyzing one's thoughts are the keys to changing attitudes. I'm sure that many are successful with their own clients, but I've seen very quick results in both behavior and attitude using my behavioral techniques. Parents appreciate the practical, commonsense ideas and love the quick turnaround they see in their kids.

The second most commonly asked question is, "Isn't this bribing my child to do what he should be doing just because he's part of this family?" The answer is unequivocally yes. He should be taking out the trash, doing his homework, and speaking politely to you because that's just good sense and common courtesy. But if he's not, and if we can motivate him to do these things using behavioral techniques, why not? Most folks wouldn't go to work if they didn't get paid, and many kids don't like to complete their chores without receiving something in return. Now, what they receive doesn't have to be exorbitant—it's privileges that parents usually give their kids anyway without their having to earn them. Behavior management, once you understand it, can be the most effective, humane, and simple approach to changing your child's inappropriate behaviors and attitudes.

As in many areas of life, a habit begun early is easier to establish and tends to remain longer than one started later. That's why it's important to begin a behavior management system when your kids are little. However, I've started many kids on the system at fourteen, fifteen, and sixteen years of age. Although they grump about it, and you may have to be creative with both positive and negative consequences, it can be quite successful.

Quiz Time

You know that you need a behavior management system for your child if:

1. You are the parent of a child at least seven years of age.
2. You've tried everything you can think of to change your kid's behavior and nothing seems to work for longer than a day or two.
3. Thoughts of shipping the child to Grandma's house (for a week, a month, perhaps longer?) are becoming obsessive.
4. You're beginning to dislike your kid even though you haven't lost one ounce of love for her.
5. You feel like a bad parent, especially after reading parenting magazines in which everyone else's kid seems to respond to the experts' suggestions.
6. You've lost control. You've turned into a nag, and this is especially frightening because you see yourself becoming more like your mother every day.
7. You now understand your parents' phrase, "I only wish upon you one just like yourself."
8. You don't want to spank your child because you're afraid you'll really hurt him.
9. You feel tremendous guilt when punishing your daughter even though you know she deserves it and will probably learn a good lesson from the consequence.
10. You're still trying to "reason with the unreasonable," trying to talk your child into seeing things your way, even though the last 101 lectures didn't make a dent.

Said yes to a bunch of these? Then you're the perfect parent for a behavior management system.

Behavior Management Techniques

I have found that kids as young as seven years of age understand and respond to this behavior management system. Younger children may not be able to comprehend this charting system, and therefore need a behavioral program that is simpler and fits their developmental level. Grade and middle schoolers generally accept the system, but teens may think that it's silly and beneath them. Once they get a gander at the privileges and rewards that they can earn, though, most quickly buy into it.

The tricks are:

1. Be consistent. If you're not going to follow through, don't threaten.

2. Be nonchalant. If you really follow the system, you'll rarely have to scream or nag. Some kids are like donkeys. They're stubborn and may be determined to show you that chart systems and programs are a bunch of junk; they're just not going to play the game. Keep cool, and if you're consistent with the consequences, keeping a nonchalant manner as you tell them that they've lost their daily privileges because they didn't work the program, pretty soon they'll come around. Trust me—I've outlasted many a mule; it just takes time and patience.

3. Don't get scared off by the look of the chart on page 76. It's not that complicated, and after you and your child have tried it for a while, it's a piece of cake!

4. Be sure to go out and buy some poker chips and a kitchen timer at this point. You'll need both to work the system effectively.

My behavior management system involves four main sections:

1. Daily Expectations (basically chores).
2. Behavior/Attitude Bad Points (all the kid stuff that drives you nuts).
3. Criteria for a "Good Day" (what the child must do to earn his rewards).
4. Consequences for Behavior (rewards and loss of privileges).

Each of these will be explained in detail and followed by actual case studies of the behavior management system set up for two of my clients. Sample behavior management charts for grade schoolers and for middle and high schoolers are shown on pages 76 and 77 and a blank one (for you to copy and use) is given on page 78.

Daily Expectations

I'm sure that your family has various chores that you would like your children to perform, but they don't always do them on time and you have to nag, nag, nag. Generally, parents set up these expectations in some form for their children, either verbally or written on a chart. In my behavior management system the Daily Expectations are listed vertically on the chart (see example on page 76), so that parents can mark their children's accomplishments each day.

Your child is given credit with a star [★] on the chart if the chore has been completed *correctly, on time,* and *without a hassle.* If the chore is not completed correctly, on time, and cooperatively, your kid then receives an X and is still made to perform the chore. This teaches him that he will still have to complete the chore but will not receive credit unless he does it without a hassle. This generally motivates kids to be cooperative with their chores, since they know they will have to do them anyway.

Grade School Behavior Management Chart

Name_____ Week of _____

Daily Rewards		Weekly Rewards	Codes
25¢ Poker Chip	*Parent Time (15 min.)*	*Needs at least five Good Days:*	★ = *On Time*
Electricity	*Grab Bag Prize*	*(1) Stay up later*	★ = *Correctly*
Playtime	*Bedtime 8:00 or 9:00 P.M.*	*(2) One special activity*	★ = *No Hassle*
Bedtime Snack	*Privilege Poker Chip*		X = *No Star*
			✔ = *Bad Point*

Daily Expectations	Sat	Sun	Mon	Tue	Wed	Thu	Fri
Go to bed well	★	★	★	★			
Get dressed (5 min.)	★	★	★	★			
Make bed (5 min.)	★	★	★	★			
Put PJ's away	X	★	★	★			
Brush teeth and hair	★	★	★	★			
Eat breakfast well	★	★	X	★			
Be home by 6 P.M.	★	★	X	★			
Daily report card	★	★	★	X			
Homework done well	★	★	★	★			
Daily chore	X	★	★	★			
House pickup (5 min.)	★	★	X	X			
Clean bedroom (5 min.)	★	X	X	★			
Bathe & clean bathroom	★	X	★	★			

Bad Points (allow 6 or 8)							
Not doing as told		✔	✔	✔✔✔			
Not taking "no" well	✔	✔		✔			
Talking back	✔						
Interrupting							
Fighting/Teasing				✔✔			
Tattling		✔					
Fussing		✔		✔			

Good Day? Needs at least 11 ★'s and 6/8 or less Bad Points							
★ = Good Day X = Bad Day	★	★	X	X			

Middle and High School Behavior Management Chart

Name_____ **Week of** _____

Daily Rewards	Weekly Rewards	Codes
Red Allowance Poker Chip *White Privilege Poker Chip* *Blue Clothing Poker Chip* *Electricity* *Freedom*	*Needs at least five Good Days:* *Normal Weekend Privileges*	★ = *On Time* ★ = *Correctly* ★ = *No Hassle* X = *No Hassle* ✔ = *Bad Point*

Daily Expectations	Sat	Sun	Mon	Tue	Wed	Thu	Fri
Go to bed without hassle	★	★	★	★			
Leave for school on time	★	★	★	★			
Make bed	★	★	★	★			
Daily assignment sheet	★	★	X	★			
Homework completed	★	★	★	★			
Chore completed by 5 P.M.	X	★	★	★			
House pickup (5 min.)	★	★	X	X			
Clean bedroom (5 min.)	★	X	X	★			
Clean up bathroom	★	X	★	★			
Bad Points (allow 6 or 8)							
Not doing as told	✔✔	✔✔	✔	✔			
Not taking "no" well		✔✔	✔	✔			
Talking back	✔		✔	✔			
Interrupting	✔			✔			
Teasing		✔✔		✔			
Bad language		✔		✔			
Rudeness		✔					
Breaking curfew		✔					
Good Day? Needs at least 7 ★'s and 6/8 or less Bad Points							
★ = Good Day X = Bad Day	★	X	X	★			

Behavior Management Chart

Name_____ Week of _____

Daily Rewards	Weekly Rewards	Codes
		★ = On time ★ = Correctly ★ = No hassle X = No Hassle ✔ = Bad Point

Daily Expectations	Sat	Sun	Mon	Tue	Wed	Thu	Fri

Bad Points (allow ___ or___)	Sat	Sun	Mon	Tue	Wed	Thu	Fri

Good Day? Needs at least ___ ★'s and ___ / ___ or less Bad Points							
★ = Good Day X = Bad Day							

Chores that parents are concerned with can range from the general to the very specific. When starting a behavior management system, I suggest that the chart be made as straightforward and specific as possible. Giving a kid a gray area is like playing Russian roulette, so leave little ambiguity regarding what is to be accomplished.

The list below is quite detailed, perhaps more so than is necessary for your family. These expectations are typical, and you can individualize the Daily Expectations for your own needs. Grade-school kids tend to have more hygiene tasks, and teens need to focus more on household chores such as cleaning the kitchen, bathroom, and bedroom areas.

Examples of Daily Expectations for Grade Schoolers

- Go to bed the night before in a cooperative manner
- Get up on time
- Get dressed (five minutes)
- Make bed (five minutes)
- Put pajamas away (five minutes)
- Brush teeth, wash face, brush hair
- Clean up after breakfast
- Leave for school on time and without complaining
- Put book bag away after school
- Complete homework cooperatively and completely
- Come in by 6:00 P.M. from outside play
- Dinner chores
- House pickup (ten minutes)
- Bedroom cleanup (ten minutes)
- Put clothes out for the next day
- Take a shower and clean up the bathroom
- Brush teeth

Examples of Daily Expectations for Middle/High Schoolers

- Go to bed without a hassle
- Make bed
- Leave for school on time
- Daily assignment sheet
- Homework completed
- Daily chore completed by _____ o'clock
- House pickup (5 minutes)
- Clean bedroom (5 minutes)
- Clean up bathroom

As may be noted from the above lists, some of the chores have time limits. As I've mentioned, a kitchen timer, an inexpensive device that can be bought at most grocery stores, is an invaluable asset for use in the behavior management system. Your child's idea of completing a chore in a timely manner is often quite different from yours. Therefore, you start the timer when the chore is to begin. For example, tell your daughter, "I am going to set the timer for bedroom cleanup. You have exactly ten minutes to clean up your room. Go!" She then has ten minutes to completely clean up the bedroom. Be sure that you have previously discussed with her what a "clean bedroom" means: there is no junk left on the floor, what was on the floor is not stuffed in the closet or under the bed, all drawers are closed, and the desktop is fairly neat. You do not expect her to dust or vacuum every day, but the bedroom is to be neat and orderly.

If upon your inspection after the timer rings you see a sneaker in one corner of the room, she must then put the shoe in the closet, but she receives an X on her chart since the task was not performed completely and on time. I know this sounds picky, but if you allow one shoe out today, trust me, there will be two left out tomorrow. Or if she finishes the task in twelve minutes rather than ten, she is not given credit since the time limit was not met.

I have made the Daily Expectation portion of the chart quite rigid. The "Be home by 6:00 P.M." Daily Expectation is an example of this. It means 6:00 P.M. on the kitchen clock, not on the child's watch (which your child can always set five minutes late). When beginning the behavior management system, all the Daily Expectations must be defined and explained thoroughly to your child so that there is no question as to what he should do to receive a star. Also, decide whether the child is expected to remember to check the chart throughout the day and perform the chores without being told, or whether you will remind him to do them. Generally, parents begin the system willing to remind kids of their chores, and after a few weeks tell them that from now on they will have to check the chart themselves and be responsible for completing their tasks each day without reminders.

The space for a Daily Expectation is never left blank. Your child either completed the chore on time, correctly, and cooperatively, and received a star, or he received an X for that item by not having completed it appropriately. If the chore is not applicable that day, such as "no homework assignment for Saturday," your child receives a free star for that space on the chart.

Behavior/Attitude Bad Points

Now for the stuff that really drives parents crazy—your child's attitude. In the Behavior/Attitude section, kids are given Bad Points [✔] for inappropriate behaviors or attitudes that you wish to decrease. Your kid is allowed a designated maximum number of Bad Points per day.

When parents are first starting this system, I suggest that they allow six Bad Points on a school day and eight Bad Points on a weekend or holiday, since the kid is with them for a greater amount of time on those days. Your child should keep the number of Bad Points to the allotted maximum amount or less in order to maintain a "Good Day" (to be discussed below). I encourage you to be fairly strict in giving out Bad Points, since if your son feels that you will look the other way, the system will be ineffective. For example, if the problem behavior is talking back, and you feel that your son spoke inappropriately but your spouse did not perceive it as such, I suggest that the child be given a "talking back" Bad Point. In this way, he will understand that you will not tolerate talking back or any other inappropriate verbal behavior, even if one of you is not as offended as the other.

Examples of Behavior/Attitude Bad Points for Grade Schoolers

- Not doing as told the first time (you having to nag the kid)
- Not taking no for an answer (the kid nagging you)
- Talking back
- Rudeness (encompasses everything from purposeful burping noises to not answering when spoken to)
- Fighting/Teasing
- Interrupting
- Tattling
- Going out to play without telling a parent
- Using things without permission
- Lying
- Stealing

Examples of Behavior/Attitude Bad Points for Middle/High Schoolers

- Not doing as told the first time
- Not taking no for an answer
- Talking back
- Rudeness
- Interrupting
- Leaving without permission
- Using things without permission

- Fighting, teasing, tattling
- Lying
- Stealing
- Cursing

These lists address the most frequent parental complaints and causes for reprimands I see in my practice. Your family may decide to delete some and add others. As you can see, it is only the tip of the iceberg in terms of possible inappropriate behaviors!

Here is an example of "not doing as told the first time": Dad tells Mark to put his magazines in his bedroom. Mark responds, "In a minute, Dad," but does not move. Dad notes, "That's one," as he puts a small check mark next to the "not doing as told the first time" row on the chart. Dad then says to Mark, "You've got one, now put your magazines in your bedroom." Mark doesn't even bother to respond this time. (Sound familiar?) Dad places a second check mark in the same row on the chart and says, "Mark, that's two. Now put your magazines in the bedroom." Mark now retorts, "I said in a minute, Dad!" and still makes no movement toward the magazines. Dad notes, "Mark, that's three," and puts the third mark on the chart.

If Mark does not comply by the third request, then he most likely will not comply upon the tenth one. Therefore, if your child receives three Bad Points *in a row,* he should be placed in time-out for at least ten minutes in an effort to break the stubbornness of the moment. Upon leaving the time-out situation, the magazine issue is revisited, and Mark again has the choice to comply or to be obstinate and receive more Bad Points.

I use this example to show how a kid can rack up several Bad Points for the *same inappropriate behavior* in quick succession. You should not be afraid to give Bad Points when your kids deserve them. Remember, you're in charge and are the keeper of the chart! If a child earns a Bad Day because of too many Bad Points, he may feel that he has nothing more to lose and may misbehave for the rest of the day. To avoid this manipulation, set the rule that if he gets nine Bad Points on a school day or eleven on a weekend or holiday, he must go to his room for the remainder of the day. That usually takes care of the problem handily.

Severe offenses such as lying and stealing can be given an automatic three or four Bad Points for each incident. Exaggerations may be seen as one Bad Point, but your daughter telling you that she had to stay after school for a soccer match when in reality she stayed for a detention is a lie; that may be worth three or four Bad Points. This is an individual decision that your family needs to make as you are developing the Bad Point section of the behavior management system. However you decide on the guidelines, make sure to be consistent!

Another area of considerable concern for parents is fighting and teasing behaviors that are often based in sibling rivalry. Most families have come to recognize that siblings fight and that they fight constantly. If they are not fighting, then they are teasing. Kids love to fight—I'm convinced that it is the sport of childhood. The only trouble is that their bickering drives us nuts! It is helpful, though, to put yourself in your kids' shoes when trying to understand sibling battles. In *Siblings Without Rivalry: How to Help Your Children Live Together So You Can Live Too,* Adele Faber and Elaine Mazlish masterfully provide this learning experience: "Imagine that your spouse puts an arm around you and says, 'Honey, I love you so much, and you're so wonderful that I've decided to have another wife just like you.'" It's often difficult for kids to share you and their stuff with a sibling, just as you would find it a bit difficult to share your spouse!

When a parent asks who started the fight, the response is usually that the other guy began it, and then an argument begins. To avoid this senseless situation, my fighting and teasing rule is: "Anybody involved in a fight or a tease receives a Bad Point." To further establish that you do not wish to hear about fighting and teasing, your kids are told that the person who tattles about the fight receives an additional Bad Point on the line marked "tattling." This rule has been known to virtually stop fighting, teasing, and tattling in just a few days. Amazing the power of Bad Points!

Inform your kids that it's okay to tell you if a sibling is doing something illegal or dangerous. That's not tattling, it's looking out for the welfare of the sibling. However, most tattling incidents involve the continuation of a fight or tease and generally serve no purpose. An additional tattling Bad Point following the fighting Bad Point usually calms down the situation.

I have noticed that most sibling battles occur out of boredom or because children enjoy fighting. If they begin to receive Bad Points for this behavior, fighting generally becomes less intriguing. This rigid fighting/teasing/tattling rule generally results in children either fighting quietly, fighting when you are not around, or more appropriate, beginning to fight less since it is just not worth it!

Criteria for a Good Day

The criteria in order to achieve a "Good Day" on the behavior management system is that your child needs to have performed adequately in both the Daily Expectation section and the Behavior/Attitude Bad Point section. A Good Day involves achieving at least a minimum number of stars on the Daily Expectation section, such as eleven out of a possible thirteen chores completed appropriately. This indicates that the child has given a good effort to complete her chores.

In addition, your kid must keep the number of Bad Points to the maximal allowable level or fewer (for example, six Bad Points or fewer on a school day or eight Bad Points or fewer on the weekend). Thus she will have to achieve the criteria in *both* the Daily Expectations and Behavior/Attitude Bad Points sections in order to earn a Good Day star at the bottom of the chart. The Good Day star line is found underneath the Behavior/Attitude Bad Points section. This line is never left blank—there will either be a star for a Good Day or an X for a Bad Day. See the sample charts on pages 76 and 77.

You can declare a Bad Day at any time. For instance, if your child received his ninth Bad Point at 2:00 on Saturday afternoon, then at that moment he knows his chart will be marked with an X in the Good Day category. At that time he is told that there will be no more Daily Rewards for the remainder of the day. If he has received some rewards prior to 2:00 P.M., there is nothing that you can do about it. Just focus on making certain that he receives no further Daily Rewards that day. If your child achieves a Good Day star on the chart near bedtime, he receives all of the Daily Rewards as discussed below.

Consequences

The rewards and punishments are divided into Daily Rewards and Weekly Rewards.

Daily Rewards

The Daily Rewards are listed on the top left side of the chart, and the Weekly Rewards are listed in the center of the chart.

In setting up the Daily Rewards, refer back to the activity, social, and material rewards discussed in Chapter 5. Your child is often the best source of ideas for these, because different kids find different things rewarding. Generally, younger children desire food treats, grab bag prizes (trinkets), stickers, and television privileges. Middle and high schoolers tend to enjoy snacks, television and video privileges, staying up later at night, and access to the telephone. It should be noted that a core principle of behavior management is to offer what is appealing to your kid, not necessarily what you feel to be important. (Remember the last of the four C's—that of *catastrophic consequences?*)

Some Daily Rewards are enticing to children but can be somewhat difficult for parents to provide. One such reward is that of "parent time." This involves your child's earning fifteen minutes of one parent's time in the evening when that parent must play any game that the child wishes to play. Children enjoy this tremendously, but it may be difficult for you to do. However, if you offer this as a reward for your child, you should be consistent and be willing to provide it.

Rewarding Responsibility

Troy and Lindsay's Mom

My son, Troy, is near the top of his class at the United States Air Force Academy. He is self-disciplined and able to take orders. This has not always been the case! In fact, if someone had told us when Troy was in fifth grade that he was destined for success as a military officer, we would have laughed hysterically. Troy was the epitome of the bright, strong-willed child. He was an A student with good behavior at home, but he acted up at school and at church.

When Dr. Peters did a psychological and intellectual profile of Troy, she noticed that even his good behavior at home required constant nagging. She suggested that we adopt the infamous (to Troy) "chart," which is still talked about in our family. It was the beginning of our short but very effective experiment with the behavior modification system that changed our family dynamics and helped both Troy and his younger sister, Lindsay, develop self-discipline.

We won't kid you. At first it took much more time to adhere faithfully to the chart than it had previously taken to nag. We had to put aside much of our own agendas as parents for a while. There was a lot of resistance from both children, especially Lindsay. Her rationale was, "I'm already good. Why do I have to do the chart?" I must admit, we never did explain that very well, except to tell her that it was "a family thing."

The biggest challenge we faced was trying to come up with enough rewards, because our family never watched much TV, and the children weren't into music, telephone, or sleepovers. We already went to restaurants and movies and played games and sports together. Troy and Lindsay felt somewhat punished to have these activities tied in with their behavior.

Our family followed the chart for about six months until the behaviors, activities, and rewards became second nature for all of us. We knew that it was time to phase out the record keeping when Troy no longer bothered to turn in his poker chips for rewards. He was satisfied with his accomplishments, behavior, and self-discipline for their own sake. In fact, until he began playing poker in high school, he refused to part with his chips! We kept a pared-down version of the chart for another six months. However, we used the system of negotiated consequences and rewards into high school for things like car privileges, dating, etc. No one missed the nagging less than Mom!

Troy and Lindsay groan when asked about the chart, but both young adults are now self-disciplined and confident achievers.

Another powerful incentive is that of poker chips. As noted in Chapter 5, kids work for material rewards, and poker chips are a convenient way to keep track of this. White poker chips can be used for privilege rewards, for example, with the child cashing in ten chips to go to the park, seven for a friend to spend the night, or four chips to stay up one half hour later to watch television.

Blue poker chips can be used for clothing purchases. Teens especially like to accumulate clothing poker chips so they can buy clothes that you may feel to be unnecessary but that they deem vital in keeping up with their friends, including rock group T-shirts or other trendy articles of clothing. You and your child should establish the monetary value of each poker chip so that it can be traded in for money at the time she goes to the store to buy the clothing. This can be one of the most effective consequences for middle and high schoolers.

Kids hate to be bored and love to be entertained, so electricity (TV, stereo, telephone, video games, and other electronics) is a very powerful behavior modifier. Electricity is a privilege, not a "given," and kids should have to earn it. Remember—electricity is anything that uses batteries or needs to be plugged in.

Another effective reward for kids is that of a daily allowance. Most parents, if they were to calculate what they spend on their child weekly, would be amazed at how much they give their kids for candy, gum, soft drinks, and other junk. Children can be incredibly persistent and can hassle you into buying them almost anything when you're shopping. Therefore, if your child can earn a red daily allowance poker chip, he can use this money to buy these items if he wishes.

For example, a fourteen-year-old may earn a two-dollar-a-day allowance, whereas an eight-year-old may receive one dollar a day. When the eight-year-old is at the grocery store and insists upon buying a comic book, you can suggest that he use his own money if he really wants it. Sometimes the child will decide to use his money and make the purchase, but you will be surprised at how often the youngster will begin to think about the necessity of such purchases when the money comes out of his own pocket! Using an allowance as a reward can be a very good learning experience for kids. It helps them appreciate the value of money while it stops arguments in stores.

Weekly Rewards

Weekly Rewards are earned if your child receives at least five Good Days out of seven during the week. A week technically begins on Saturday morning and ends Friday night. Weekly Rewards include enjoying normal weekend privileges, such as staying up later on Friday and Saturday nights, having a friend spend the night, going skating, going to the movies, or picking which restaurant to go to for dinner.

If a Good Week has not been earned, your child does not get to stay up later on Friday and Saturday nights. She is not grounded, but she may not socialize out of the neighborhood (a predetermined area) during the weekend. You should make the weekend as boring as possible so that this consequence has a significant effect on your kid.

This brings up a typical kid comment when they begin my behavior management system. Some complain that they will now have to work for items and activities that were previously just handed to them. For example, many kids are allowed to stay up later on weekends, have friends spend the night, go to the mall, and receive allowances without having to accomplish any tasks. When the behavior management system begins, they now have to complete chores and behave appropriately. Some kids react negatively to this because they feel they are not getting anything extra out of the deal. Your most effective response to this behavior is to note that *you* are going to adhere to the rules of the behavior management system and if your son does not want to, it's his choice, but he will not receive his Daily or Weekly Rewards. End of subject!

Some very stubborn kids will decide not to go along with the program for a week or two, but after they see that they are not receiving their allowance, they have no television or telephone privileges, and they are not allowed to see their friends, then most *will* begin to cooperate.

It may be difficult to control television and telephone use, but I've found creative ways to make sure that you can monitor these activities. Many families I've worked with will remove these items from the child's bedroom, making it harder for him to sneak use. I've even had some folks flip the circuit breaker to the child's bedroom (assuming that this doesn't interfere too much with other family members) and then put a lock on the circuit breaker box so the child cannot go to the garage when they're gone and flip the switch on.

However, I suggest to parents of physically aggressive kids that they *do not* get into a battle with their child over negative consequences. A teenager can easily intimidate Mom, especially if he is bigger and stronger than she. I suggest in these cases, for example, that if the kid uses TV without permission and you can't disconnect it or take it away (it may be the one in the family room that everybody watches), then you note the infraction and add an additional punishment later.

For instance, you might give away one of your child's CDs or cassette tapes, or maybe even a favorite article of clothing. Obviously you shouldn't take the item when the child is still angry. This should be done in a controlled manner. For instance, set the rule "If you continue to use television after you have earned a Bad Day, I will not fight with you about it. At the first safe opportunity I will take one of your possessions and give it away. It's your choice, but I will not fight with you if you continue to break a rule. I will take action when it is safe to do so."

Another time when you may wish to take away a possession occurs if you send your kid to time-out and she refuses to go. Again, no fisticuffs here, because someone may get hurt. Say to your daughter, "You've earned fifteen minutes of time-out and you are refusing to go. I cannot make you go, and I'm certainly not going to try to physically drag you into your room. Instead I'm setting the timer for two minutes. If you are not in the bathroom for time-out by the time the buzzer goes off, then when it is convenient and safe, I will take one of your possessions and give it away. It's your choice. I'm setting the timer now."

What do you do if one of your kids earns a Weekly Reward and the other one doesn't? This is an excellent learning situation for both children. The child who has earned the Weekly Reward should receive it, and the child who hasn't should not. For example, the kid with the Good Week may choose to go roller skating. The one with the Bad Week can either remain at home or go to the skating rink, but is not allowed to participate. Either way, both children will see that their behavior affects what happens to them, which is the whole point of behavior management. Generally this does not increase sibling resentment, but rather motivates the child who did not earn the Weekly Reward to make sure that next time he will get it as well.

The Chart in Action

Jackie, Casey, and Richie's Mom

I have three children. My two daughters, Jackie and Casey, have been for the most part well behaved. Time-outs and taking away privileges have worked well when needed. I felt quite successful as a mom. My third child, Richie, is handsome and smart, with a great sense of humor. Unfortunately, every possible method of punishment I used with the girls did not work on him.

Richie was a difficult baby. He had colic, nursed every two hours, and did not sleep for more than two or three hours at a time. If I put him down he would scream, so I carried him everywhere. As Richie grew, he became more demanding and strong-willed, and if he didn't get his way, he would explode. I tried everything. Time-out was a joke—I would have to physically hold him in his chair. Sometimes he would try to hit or kick me. I couldn't believe this precious child of mine was behaving this way.

I didn't handle the situation very well. I threatened, bribed, begged, cried, and spanked. I found myself ignoring a lot of the bad behavior because I found that compromise was the only way to get Richie to do anything. This frustrated and angered my husband, who thought I was too lenient. He is a pediatrician, so he thought we should know how to handle Richie better, and our relationship became increasingly stressed. I began to believe that I was a terrible mom. Why were we so unsuccessful with our youngest child?

I decided to seek professional help, and Dr. Peters was recommended to me. I was willing to try anything. During our first visit Dr.

Peters asked Richie and me very detailed questions. So detailed that I didn't know the answers! Where do you want Richie to put his night clothes, in the hamper or on the dresser? I really didn't care, as long as they weren't on the floor! Richie described his daily routine, and together we developed a plan that listed nine chores and desired behaviors for Richie. I had been afraid to expect Richie to do any chores because of the hassle we went through, but because Richie's input was requested throughout the interview, he felt that he had a stake in the chart. Richie told Dr. Peters that he would do nine chores a day, and he especially loved the idea of Daily Rewards. But I was skeptical.

I liked several things about the system. Details, details, details. Richie knew exactly what he was supposed to do to get a star for a particular chore. Richie often said he would pick up his toys "in a minute," but of course he never actually did it. With the chart, Richie was given five minutes to pick up the mess in the family room, and he had five minutes to start his homework after his snack break. He also had the choice not to do two of the chores in the beginning. This gave him power. The program was forgiving, but only a little bit.

The behavior section of the chart was my favorite and Richie's least favorite section. When I gave Richie his first Bad Point, he fell apart. He cried and threatened. He said he hated the program and wasn't going to do it ever again. My fears returned, but I hung in there. I tried to remain calm and reassured Richie that he had five more chances to mess up before he lost all his Daily Rewards. This settled him slightly, but I found myself scared to give the next Bad Point.

Richie absolutely loved the Daily Rewards section of the chart. Dr. Peters included him in deciding what the rewards would be, and money and baseball cards were the most important things to him. Richie wasn't sure about the privilege and clothing poker chips, but was willing to receive them anyway. He had a lot of success with the chart the first week. A few times since then Richie has chosen not to complete his chores. He knows the consequences. At night Richie wishes he had done the chores, but he knows he must accept his choice.

My daughters have resisted the behavior management program because they feel that they are well behaved and that the system is intended for younger children. But I did put them on a modified program. They are expected to clean their rooms daily, put their stuff away after school, and help me when asked. If they fight with each other, all involved get a Bad Point. Now they are beginning to accept the program, especially since they are receiving chips consistently—I often forgot to give them their allowance in the past.

Life has not been perfect, but it has been so much better. I am not losing my temper nearly as much, and I am not nagging, begging, and spanking as often. Richie still loses it sometimes, threatening that he will not continue to do the chart, but it usually lasts only a few minutes. The privilege chips have been fun—Richie saves them for trips to the hobby store, baseball card shows, etc. I have made an effort to do special things with Richie, and it really has been enjoyable. Our lives have settled down and we are getting along much better. Most important, I am feeling better about being a mom.

Richie

I like the behavior management system because it is good for a lot of people, including me. My favorite part is when I get my baseball cards and money chips. I get Bad Points if I don't do my chores or if I misbehave, which is not good. Since we have been on the program we don't fight as much. Mom doesn't yell at me to get me to do something. I really like getting rewards every night. It is also fair because if I mess up a little bit it's okay. Sometimes I decide I don't want to do my chores, and then I don't get my chips. I used to get punished sometimes for several days, but now I start fresh every day, which I like. I hope other kids do this chart, too.

It's tough to be consistent, and your children may try to manipulate you into disregarding the charting system. However, if you dig your heels in and remain consistent, you should see excellent results within a few weeks, and the program *will become self-rewarding.*

It's important that you realize the behavior management system involves your child's relationship with her own behavior through the chart and is not based upon your whims or moods. If this is followed, she will begin to take more responsibility for her own actions. Saying, "Because you have earned a Good Day on the chart, here are your rewards," reinforces the cause/effect relationship between the kid's behavior and the consequences that will occur.

Playing Hardball

Once in a while I run into a kid who is so stubborn that he is stoically willing to accept the "standard" negative consequences of the behavior management system without flinching. These kids continue to have Bad Days even though this means losing privileges such as freedom and electricity, as well as their daily allowance and clothing money.

With this type of kid I often recommend playing hardball, which means beefing up the consequences and even adding others, so that the total package becomes so intense that it just isn't worth being stubborn anymore. The child usually gives in and plays ball—and good behavior follows. So now for some hardball ideas:

As noted earlier, time-outs begin at ten minutes long and can be lengthened for five- or ten-minute intervals as needed. It is not unusual for kids to earn time-outs for thirty, sixty, or ninety minutes, especially when they are exceptionally ornery. Some kids push the system to the point of needing time-out from the moment they get home from school until dinner, or from after dinner until bedtime. Others even have to go to time-out from the moment they come home from school until bedtime. This will get any kid's attention, and they will finally give in and work with the system if they believe that they will have to face several hours of boredom in the time-out room.

The time-out spot is also negotiable. In Chapter 5, I discussed time limits and the best location for time-out, and you may want to review that section. If you find that the time-out spot you are using is not effective, you may want to consider using bathroom time-out. If you do, make sure that the bathroom is well lit and ventilated and that it is safe—pills, scissors, and other potentially dangerous objects removed. Remember—boredom is one of the most powerful tools to use with your child. He will work hard to avoid it, even if it means doing things he doesn't want to do.

Taking away a prized possession and donating it to the Salvation Army, Goodwill, or a shelter for underprivileged kids can often be the negative consequence that turns the tide. Many parents have tried the tactic of temporarily removing a possession that the child will get or earn back after a specified amount of time has passed or cessation of the inappropriate behavior occurs. My experience has shown me that kids are rarely fazed if they know they can get the item back. Plenty of Nintendo cartridges and bicycles are "put away" and returned within a few weeks, but the child is quite adaptable. Just knowing that he'll get his things back eases the pain. However, realizing that he'll never see his favorite CD again will definitely get your son's attention, and he may think twice before talking back the next time. If he's really obstinate, it may take losing his entire CD collection and a few of his favorite shirts before he caves in and watches how he speaks to you.

Most parents, however, have a philosophical conflict with giving away their kids' possessions. This stuff costs a lot of money, and they are reluctant to just give it away. When this issue comes up, I usually remind them of my hourly fee, pointing out that losing a few CDs doesn't even come close to the cost of therapy. If that doesn't sway them, I paint the picture of what life will be like with an even brattier kid if they don't get a handle on the youngster's behavior now.

Often I describe actual cases to my clients, showing them how other kids in our community have landed in situations such as Juvenile Court, foster care, or residential treatment centers because parents lost control of their children's behavior. Not cleaning their room is no big deal, but constantly disobeying, engaging in illegal activities, and showing disrespect for authority are biggies, and parents need to do whatever is necessary to get their kid's behavior under control. Generally, that's enough to convince parents to give away possessions, and once they see how effective it is, they often become true believers in this tactic.

Behavior management is also effective for school problems. Teachers can use charts for out-of-seat behavior, talking too much, rudeness, and other inappropriate actions in the classroom. You can discuss your behavior management program with your child's teachers and help them set up something similar in the school setting.

Most of the time kids respond beautifully to behavioral systems. Perhaps for the first time their parents have a game plan—a set of rules that every family member acknowledges and has to live with. Kids thrive on structure. If you are an unstructured person, it will be a challenge to work with a charting system. But you can do it, and I'm sure your home life will be calmer, more controlled, and more comfortable for everyone!

One of the nicest features of behavioral techniques is that the program, once successful, can easily be modified later to a simpler system. One family I know has evolved from the charting system to a very simple poker chip program. Both kids are given two poker chips a day, worth one dollar each. Mom and Dad remove a chip each time a child *does anything inappropriate*—talks back, argues, fights with sibling, doesn't get a chore done well, etc. This very simple plan has worked well for this family for over ten years, mainly because the kids want the money and they know that their parents will be consistent and remove the chip.

However, the simple poker chip system wouldn't have been appropriate to start with. The kids needed a behavior management chart delineating specific chores and attitudes for at least the first year. Once these behaviors became second nature, the simpler poker chip system was instituted. It's easy to use and it works!

Behavior Management Case Studies

Brandon

Brandon's case is a typical one that illustrates the plight of many parents. Brandon had been a beautiful, easygoing baby. His parents, Claire and Mike, felt that parenthood was not going to be as much of a chore as their friends and relatives had predicted. Brandon slept through the night before the end of his third month, nursed easily, and took to solid foods very well. He always had a quick smile, and even though he "seemed to be into everything," the loving way about the little boy melted their hearts.

It wasn't until the beginning of Brandon's fourth year that Claire and Mike became concerned about his behavior. They had given him everything they could materially as well as their time and attention. Brandon, their first and at that time only child, was not in want for anything.

About the time of his fourth birthday, the parents noted that his behavior was becoming very demanding. In fact, he threw a temper tantrum at his birthday party in front of his playmates and family because he didn't receive a certain piece of cake. In order to quiet Brandon down, Mike traded cake plates with one of Brandon's friends so that he received the piece that he desired. That seemed to work, but Brandon was still grumpy following the incident.

Later that night, Mike and Claire discussed Brandon's behavior. Claire tended to feel that he had misbehaved due to the excitement stimulated by his birthday presents, family, and other guests, but Mike was not sure. Mike had begun to see a trend in the evenings when he returned home from work. Claire seemed to be frazzled and upset with Brandon's behavior. She generally met Mike at the door looking very tired, and there were more and more evenings when Claire would list Brandon's transgressions over dinner. She was frustrated and felt guilty about her relationship with her son.

Brandon would whine and complain when he was told no, and

Claire would resort to almost anything to quiet him. The usual distractions (tickling, food treats) did not seem to work as well as they had when he was a toddler. Brandon would stand his ground, and had begun to bite and kick when his demands were not immediately met.

Claire had tried reasoning with the youngster, explaining why she had to say no to him on occasion. She had even sent him to his room once, but Brandon kept coming out. Claire finally relented and gave him what he had originally wanted.

Mike was supportive of his wife since he did not know what to do either. This pattern of behavior increased to the time when Brandon entered kindergarten. In school, the teachers noted that he had difficulty remaining on tasks that he didn't like to do and would become disruptive to other children when he was bored.

Sitting in a circle and listening to his teacher read was a very difficult task for Brandon, especially if the teacher was not reading a book that he particularly liked. He tended to have difficulty getting along with other youngsters, since they did not cater to his needs, and his evaluations at parent/teacher conferences were becoming more and more negative. When he was in first grade, the school conferences became even worse. Claire and Mike were willing to do anything that the school asked, but no one seemed to know what to do to make Brandon behave.

At home, Brandon began to throw even more tantrums when he did not get his way. By the time Brandon was seven years old and in second grade, Mike had begun to spank the child. This only seemed to anger Brandon and didn't change his behavior.

About this time, Claire found out that she was pregnant again, and her happiness about the new baby was somewhat diminished because she feared that the new child might behave like Brandon. She and Mike worried that they would have to deal with two demanding, noncompliant youngsters. Claire was also concerned that Brandon might hurt the baby during a tantrum.

It was during Claire's pregnancy that she and Mike began to talk to their pediatrician about getting help for the family. The pediatrician asked several questions about Brandon's response to discipline. Claire and Mike felt certain that no amount of discipline was going to help with their son. The pediatrician then recommended psychological counseling with me in order to help them take back control of the situation.

It took Claire and Mike several weeks to decide to call, because they were not sure that anyone could help with their disruptive son. The final straw came when Brandon began to talk back to his second-grade teacher and refused to come in from the playground at the end of recess. The school had asked the parents to consider placing him in a special educational program for noncompliant children. That seemed to be the catalyst that Mike and Claire needed in order to get help from a psychologist.

The family came to see me, and we set about developing a behavior management system. Brandon initially questioned why he would have to work for rewards that he had previously received automatically, and because of that he felt that my system was unfair. I told him that he could earn even more privileges if he chose to behave appropriately.

His parents were especially interested in establishing chores and expectations for Brandon, but they doubted that he would cooperate. I told them to take a positive attitude and to expect Brandon to achieve his Daily Expectations. His behavior would be a barometer of their own consistency in following the chart.

We focused on Brandon's inappropriate behaviors of talking back, not doing as told the first time, and not taking no for an answer. Brandon had an incredible ability to argue when he was not given his way, and his folks desperately needed to control his stubbornness. Mike and Claire also suggested giving Bad Points for interrupting, complaining, fussing, and tantrumming.

Mike questioned what would happen if Brandon lost his Good

Day star at 3:00 P.M. on Saturday and realized he had lost all of his Daily Rewards. He speculated that Brandon would probably misbehave for the remainder of the day, since he had nothing more to lose.

I suggested that if Brandon lost the Good Day star and continued to earn more Bad Points, he would immediately go to his bedroom for the remainder of the day. Brandon would come out for dinner and his bath, but would spend the rest of the day in his bedroom. The purpose of this rule is to discourage children from abusing the system. Kids like Brandon are so manipulative that once they lose the Good Day star they may act out for the remainder of the day just to aggravate their parents.

Brandon seemed to perk up during the discussion of the Daily Rewards. He suggested food treats, allowance poker chips, and extra television privileges. In addition, he proposed Weekly Rewards of going fishing with his father and going to the park. Brandon also wished to go to a baseball trading card store periodically to spend his poker chips.

The notions of consistency and consequences, and the idea that rewards were to be earned, not just given, were somewhat foreign to both Mike and Claire. It was difficult for them to accept that they had to change some of their basic ideas regarding child rearing in order to make a better life for Brandon and for themselves. They were skeptical about the system, but they committed to following through with it.

I saw the family again in two weeks, and they brought the behavior management charts with them. Brandon had performed quite well on the Daily Expectation section, especially on those items that involved the use of a timer. Claire noted that he liked to play "beat the buzzer," and was becoming expert at making his bed and getting dressed on time by himself. In fact, Brandon was quite proud that he could now brush his teeth without his mother's assistance. His folks were amazed that Brandon could become more responsible in such a short time, and they were quite pleased with him, but they worried that the changes would only be temporary.

I explained to them that these commonsense suggestions work quickly and effectively, and lead to permanent changes if parents continue to be consistent with the consequences. Because of the simplicity of the system, it may appear that the changes are superficial and temporary, but as I have witnessed for more than twenty years, behavior management generally leads to permanent behavioral and attitudinal improvements.

Brandon was still having difficulty with the Bad Points section, especially "doing as told the first time without fussing." He often needed to be asked three times, and therefore received three Bad Points leading to a short time-out, before he would cooperate. However, in the two-week period between appointments he had earned ten Good Days out of the possible fourteen. In fact, he had received five Good Days out of the previous seven and earned the Weekly Reward of going fishing with his dad. Brandon told me of his plans for his next Weekly Reward, and Mike and Claire were only too pleased to comply with his wishes, since he was now behaving appropriately for rewards, instead of tantrumming to get what he wanted.

Brandon's behavior was still not perfect, and Mike and Claire admitted that they had allowed some Bad Points to go by without marking them on the chart. This is common when parents begin the system, and it often takes several weeks before they adjust their attitude in order to give Bad Points more accurately and quickly. I told them that the more strictly they followed the system, the better their son's behavior would be.

Over the next two months, the number of Bad Points allowed was decreased so that Brandon could get only four Bad Points on a school day and six on a weekend day. Mike and Claire did not wish to decrease the allowable number below this. They felt that they were being fairly strict with him, and that Brandon was actually behaving better than most kids they knew. Although he gave them a run for their money at times, they believed that they had adequate control over their son for the first time in many years.

Their home life had calmed down, and Brandon was going to bed without a fuss. Claire had more time for herself, and their marriage had even improved. As is seen in so many families where kids' behavior frustrates parents, when the child's behavior improves, the parents relax. With less stress in the household, Mom and Dad actually have time to talk and enjoy each other again.

As an added reward, Brandon's parents were able to relax and anticipate the arrival of their second child. Knowing that they were now capable of controlling their son's behavior gave them the confidence to expect that they could do so with Brandon's sibling as well.

Brandon was going to visit his grandmother for a week during the summer, and the chart was going with him. Mike and Claire felt that his behavior had improved so much that they were certain he would behave for Grandma as long as she used the chart.

Two months after school began, Heather was born. Although it was a hectic time, Mike and Claire continued to keep up the behavior charts. Brandon loved being a big brother and was very careful with Heather, much to his parents' relief.

Brandon remained on the behavior management system for the next six months. After that, the family was able to modify the program so that he was expected to complete "morning chores," "afternoon chores," and "evening chores." This included all of the specific chores previously expected, but he was now able to have them grouped into three periods each day. Brandon was able to handle this broader system, and it was easier for Mike and Claire to keep track of the chart. They felt much more comfortable as parents, knowing now that they were in control—not their kid. All it took was consistency, a nonchalant attitude, and a system of clear, fair rules.

Seven-year-old Brandon responded well to the new set of rules partly because he was young and his parents had control over so many aspects of his life. With teenagers it's often more difficult because they are more mobile and independent, and they have a peer group pressuring them to behave in certain ways. Often, peer pressure becomes more powerful than parents' desires, leading to stubborn standoffs between parents and kids.

One of my most difficult teens was sixteen-year-old Alana. She had not been a problem until middle school, but once she hit sixth grade her personality began to change dramatically. Two things generally occur when children go to middle school: they must now deal with six subjects each day and organize accordingly, and they are faced with incredible peer pressure.

In elementary school, Alana had a few good neighborhood girl-friends that she could count on to play with. However, when she went to sixth grade, kids began to develop cliques, and Alana began to feel that she didn't fit in with anyone.

Even though she wasn't really interested in boys, many of her classmates seemed to be infatuated with guys. They joked about sneaking into R-rated movies, taking alcohol from their parents' liquor cabinets, and even shoplifting. Although she knew these behaviors were wrong and felt uncomfortable with them, Alana chose to join a group of kids who engaged in risk-taking behaviors. These kids readily accepted her if she laughed along with them and pretended that she thought these actions were cool. Although Alana felt somewhat guilty about being with kids who bragged about these misdeeds, it felt better to belong to a crowd than to feel like an outsider.

By the middle of eighth grade, Alana was no longer just laughing at the misbehavior of her friends, she was engaging in it. She snuck out in the middle of the night to smoke cigarettes, experimented with marijuana, and slacked off in her schoolwork. Alana had also developed a new attitude with her parents—argumentative, unreasonable, and angry when her folks caught her misbehaving and would place her on restriction.

I first saw Alana after she had begun high school, and the pattern of her behavior was only getting worse. Her parents wanted to believe and trust her, yet Alana's sneaking and lying had led them to become quite suspicious and restrictive. They were at the point of believing that the only way to avoid trouble was to keep her in the house under their watchful eye.

Alana complained to me that her home life was like being in jail, and her parents had few freedoms also, since they were afraid to leave her alone. The situation was perhaps most unfair to Alana's twelve-year-old brother Peter, who couldn't go out with both his parents because someone had to stay home to watch Alana. Although his folks did things with him separately, they rarely attempted family activities because Alana was so surly that she ruined almost every occasion. The situation had deteriorated to the point that Alana's parents were considering sending her to boarding school, where the staff would be paid to watch her, and they and Peter could live a fairly normal life.

After meeting the family I explained to the parents that kids like Alana often buckle under peer pressure and behave in ways that they would never have considered before. However, the damage had been done by ninth grade, and Alana's behaviors had become bad habits. I agreed with Alana that she must be miserable and understood that she felt her parents to be unfair because they constantly grounded her.

She was able to see the connection between her sneaky behavior and their distrust, but she didn't seem to know how to break the negative cycle. Her life appeared to be one big mess, and she had little hope that she would ever get off restriction.

After hearing the family's history, the first thing I did was try to put things back into a workable perspective. Placing Alana on a month-long restriction for misdeeds just didn't work; she felt that she would never have freedom again and that consequences just didn't matter anymore. By placing the family (including Peter) on a behavior management system focusing on *daily behaviors* and *daily consequences,* Alana was given hope that if she behaved for twenty-four hours she would have some of her freedoms back. And as a bonus, Peter liked the idea of getting Daily Rewards.

We set up the Daily Expectations, including keeping her room clean, helping with the dishes, and taking care of the family dog. Alana also brought a note home from school each day, signed by each of her teachers, on which she had written her homework assignments. Schoolwork was to be completed before she could have any freedoms that day.

Bad Points centered on arguing, talking back, and rudeness. Sneaking out and lying were the two categories of behavior that had to be ceased immediately, so both were given the status of "Automatic Bad Day" if her parents caught her in a lie or leaving the house without permission. Because Alana was able to earn her freedom on a daily basis now, sneaking out of the house ceased to be a problem. Lying was more difficult for her to stop, but she began to watch what she said once she had a taste of freedom and having a Good Day became important to her.

Alana's Daily Rewards were the typical ones that most teens are interested in: freedom, money, clothing, and electricity. On a Good Day, after homework was completed and shown to her folks, she could go out until dinner, watch TV, and talk on the phone. She also received poker chips for her $2.00-per-day allowance and $1.50 per day for clothing.

Working the system was much easier for Alana than she had initially expected. Getting her chores done came easily since her parents put definite time limits on each one and Alana knew exactly what was expected of her each day. Keeping the Bad Points below the maximum allowable amount also came naturally to her. When she got her fourth or fifth Bad Point, Alana watched her behavior closely and made sure that she rarely went above number six.

The system worked for Alana because she was no longer faced with extreme penalties for extreme behaviors. Instead of feeling that she'd never have a life again, it was relatively easy for her to handle losing her privileges for one day if she did not do well. She lost her freedom, electricity, allowance, and clothing money for the day, but was able to begin with a fresh start the next morning.

Interestingly, Alana herself decided that hanging around some of her old friends wasn't worth it anymore. They tended to have little self-control themselves and encouraged her to come home late and to disregard her parents' rules. Alana realized that these kids really weren't true friends if they didn't care if she got in trouble at home and lost her privileges. She slowly began to make new friends—perhaps not as exciting as her old ones, but certainly more responsible.

Luckily, Alana was the type of child who could see that hanging with the old crowd would only get her back into trouble. However, many kids refuse to give up their friends, which poses a sticky problem for Mom and Dad. When this occurs I usually suggest a *compromise* such as:

1. The child can continue to see any friend during school.
2. Friends that parents feel comfortable with can come and go.
3. Friends that the parents are concerned about can see the child only at home where they can be supervised or under certain circumstances that the parent controls, such as going to a movie with a parent driving them.

Because Alana was behaving better at home, doing her schoolwork, and generally being civil again, her parents began to relax and to trust her more. With increased trust came more privileges, and Alana told me that over the months she was being allowed to do most of the things she wanted to.

Alana is a lucky kid—she's smart enough to realize that she has the ability to control her life and the consequences that occur to her. She's also fortunate to have parents who are able to stick with the behavior management program. They felt bad when she didn't do enough of her chores or had racked up too many Bad Points, but they followed through with the consequences we had set up.

Alana will be okay. Her folks have stopped the downward cycle of her inappropriate behavior. Her brother, Peter, also profited from this system because his expectations were clearly set out by the program and he complied well to earn the rewards that were important to him.

Obviously it's easier to begin setting rules when your kids are young. They grow up with structure and expectations naturally. However, Alana's case shows that it's also possible to do so with a teenager. You just have to be more tenacious and creative!

SPECIAL SITUATIONS:

The Miserable Wallower and the Shy Kid

The behavior management program presented in Chapter 6 focuses on typical child/adolescent behaviors and chores. However, it is not limited to problem areas such as talking back or not doing as told when told. Almost any inappropriate or ineffective behavior can be changed using this system. Many parents have brought kids in to see me for specific behaviors that, at first glance, would seem likely to respond only to traditional talk therapy and not be conducive to a behavior management approach. They may appear to be extreme emotional or social issues, or even personality problems, but I've found that almost all behavioral, social, and personality problems can be solved if treated in a behavioral fashion. Let's take a look at two of these more common child emotional problems from a behavioral perspective.

The Miserable Wallower

Even emotional areas that were once thought of as problems amenable only to talk therapy have been found to be appropriate for behavioral techniques. One of these, the *miserable wallower*, is exemplified by eleven-year-old Justin. He was brought to my office by his parents after his teacher described him as depressed and displaying a poor self-concept. Justin reportedly said "I'm stupid" or "I don't know anything" when he did poorly on tests.

When he didn't complete his chores at home and was reprimand-ed by his parents, Justin was known to allude to "doing himself in"—with comments such as "I don't know why I was born" or "Nobody likes me."

His folks were concerned that he had suicidal thoughts because he felt so poorly about himself. They described him as a kid who could perceive a trip to Disney World as a painful experience. It was as if Justin flourished in his misery. I interviewed Justin, and although he definitely looked unhappy, I wasn't sure that he was truly depressed.

I explained to Justin and his family that he had developed a per-sonality style that I call the miserable wallower—someone who has developed habits of taking constructive comments as criticism, being overly sensitive to playful teasing, and feeling rejected if not immedi-ately made the center of attention. He was terribly defensive and found it difficult to take responsibility for his own behavior. He attributed his poor grades to a lack of intelligence rather than ineffec-tive studying, and when friends shunned him because he cried when teased, it only reinforced in his mind what a worthless person he was.

Justin's parents, at a loss as to how to help him and worried that he may be suicidal, actually encouraged his negative statements about himself by giving him increased attention when he appeared to be miserable. I told them that he may look miserable, but most likely he wasn't nearly as unhappy as he portrayed himself. Justin was just *stuck*; his habits of saying negative things about himself and blaming his poor performance on "being stupid" were cop-outs. It was easier for him to wallow in self-pity than to learn to deal more effectively with other kids' teasing or to take the time to study effectively. Since his parents rewarded him for being mis-erable by giving attention and concern, Justin acted increasingly more unhappy as the years went by.

After a few futile sessions trying to talk Justin out of his mis-ery by showing him how he misinterpreted various situations in his life, I decided to use a behavioral approach. We employed a behavior management system using the Bad Point section only. Any self put-downs that he could not prove were accurate were given "negative self-statement" Bad Points. For instance, if Justin said, "I failed the test because I'm stupid," he was given a Bad Point because he had been tested the year before and told that his IQ was in the Bright Average range. Bright kids do not fail tests due to stupidity; they fail because they are unprepared. So any mention of intellectual dullness gained him no sympathy from others, only a Bad Point on his chart. When he stated that "no one likes me," he would receive a Bad Point if he wasn't able to be more specific. Questions such as "Who doesn't like you?", "What did they say?", "How did you interpret the teasing?", and "What was your reaction?" had to be answered before his parents believed that "nobody liked him." In effect, Justin was being held accountable for his sad expressions and negative statements.

I saw the family two weeks later, and they were amazed at how few Bad Points he had received in these specific areas. Because saying negative things now took a lot of effort—he had to answer several questions—and could lead to a Bad Point, Justin tended to save his negativity for times when he really felt bad about himself. His parents took his comments seriously when he could logically explain what was bothering him, and then they tried to work with him either to change his perception of the problem or to change the situation, if it truly was unfair. Although pleased with Justin's new habit of saying mainly neutral or positive things about himself, his folks were even more excited with the subtle personality changes they saw taking place in their son.

He now rarely cried for no apparent reason, and he just seemed happier. When I asked him what he thought was happening, he told me that "it was just too much trouble to be sad." It was easier to be happy now that his parents made him accountable for his negative self-statements.

Kids who appear miserable may be miserable; they can be very unhappy, lonely, and even suicidal. I always take them at their word until I evaluate what emotions truly lie behind their statements. If they are really depressed, a referral to a psychiatrist may be appropriate. However, if I feel that this emotion is based more in a pattern of having become comfortable with misery, I quickly move to a behavioral approach to reduce the negative self-statements.

Differentiating between true depression and the habit of being miserable can be tricky, and the diagnosis should be made by a counselor who is familiar with the symptoms of each. True depression is associated with definite behavioral signs such as changes in sleeping and eating patterns and social withdrawal. The miserable wallower usually doesn't display these characteristics, but tends to show a pattern of negativism following disappointments. If you're not sure which it is, check with your pediatrician for referral to a competent counselor who can make the diagnosis and recommend the most beneficial treatment. See Chapter 10 for further discussion.

Once the habitual negative statements are lessened, it is much easier to gauge what is really going on in a child's life and then to deal with it. In essence, this program shows the kid that he is not allowed to act miserable unless he truly is, and most of the time I find that children are not truly sad; they may be angry or defensive or just wallowing in old habits. Using a behavior management approach, therefore, is definitely something to consider before labeling your child as depressed and resorting to medication or more intensive treatments.

The Shy Kid

One of the most touching types of kids I see in my practice is the painfully shy. These kids are often so afraid of peer rejection that they assume anything they say to others will be perceived as inept, so they often go through the school day tongue-tied and anxious. Many of these children are lonely because making friends often involves taking interpersonal risks—a behavior that shy people just don't do well. It's a vicious cycle: afraid to talk to peers, they present themselves as awkward and different from others. Some are perceived as snobbish, while others are seen as uninvolved and perhaps a little strange.

Shy kids generally describe themselves as "invisible." Classmates wouldn't care if they didn't show up for lunch, and nobody would notice if they missed school for a week. It's interesting, though, that when surrounded by family or close friends, these same kids can relax and display their true personalities. Once the social anxiety disappears, they are often seen as witty, creative, and compassionate people. But when faced with a new group of peers, they will revert to the quiet, awkward youth, afraid of being noticed and perhaps made fun of.

Alicia, a sixteen-year-old high school sophomore, could have been a poster child for extreme shyness. Although a diligent student with excellent grades, she, like most shy kids, described herself to me as almost invisible. She often skipped lunch to avoid eating alone, preferring to spend the period in the library. Her parents tried to interest her in joining school clubs and community activities, but Alicia was a professional "yes, but" person—she had an excuse for avoiding any new social activity. I, too, tried to talk Alicia into joining activities, but shyness, like most inborn personality traits, does not respond readily to traditional talk therapy. I can't convince a teen that she is pretty, witty, or even interesting. After all, I'm just an adult, and what else am I expected to say?

We have yet to find a cure for shyness, mainly because it's a highly genetic personality trait, so deeply ingrained that environmental manipulation is often only partially successful. What lead to changes in this area are successful involvements with peers. If other high schoolers began to accept Alicia, then she would begin to accept herself—to feel more comfortable being with others and perhaps to take some social risks.

To promote social involvement, I used the Bad Points section of the behavior management program. Shyness is basically a social phobia, and to break any phobia the person has to do the opposite of what she naturally wants to do when facing the feared situation. The claustrophobic slowly places herself in smaller environments, the bridge phobic gradually drives over increasingly longer bridges, and the social phobic slowly places herself in increasingly more anxious social situations. These gradual progressions slowly allow the individual to deal effectively with greater levels of anxiety, eventually accomplishing her goal.

Alicia, her parents, and I set up a "fear gauge," with joining a new group, such as a church youth group or community service organization, gauged as a five; joining a school club, with peers that she would also see during the school day, gauged as a ten; and phoning a good acquaintance as a one. They were to fill in the remainder of the scale at home when they had more time together to do so.

Alicia was given the task of tackling the items on her fear gauge one by one. If she didn't try to use the social skills I taught her, return phone calls, or sign up for a meeting, or if she directly refused to tackle a reasonable situation, she was given Bad Points, leading to negative consequences such as losing her daily allowance and electricity. Since watching television and listening to music were the mainstays of her free time, Alicia was motivated to avoid losing these activities. She also wanted to keep her allowance and clothing poker chips so she could buy more clothes—in her mind, to fit in better with the other kids. Alicia also received Bad Points for avoiding eye contact, a trait almost always found in the very shy.

The Shy Kid

Greg's Mom

School was challenging for my son, Greg, even from the early years. His immaturity in size and social skills, along with his learning difficulties, caused him to be withdrawn around his peers. (Fortunately, his verbal acuity and good manners endeared him to adults, so he has not been without any self-confidence.)

The family moved away from his home state when he was thirteen and in middle school—definitely a difficult time for all children. Because the public school in our new town had large classes, we decided to send Greg to a small private school. There were only eighteen students in his grade. But his lack of adaptability, learning problems, and social immaturity made seventh and eighth grade very stressful. He enjoyed school and was generally happy with his teachers, but he was visibly strained at the end of the school day from the teasing by his "enemies," as he called them. He was afraid to leave his family for any overnight activities, such as field trips or camp.

High school was a friendlier place for Greg, and easier academically, too, thanks to a special learning disabilities class there. Still, Greg was reluctant to attend any activities outside of school. We sought Dr. Peters's help.

Dr. Peters convinced Greg to try managing the high school football program. As a result, he gained respect and recognition in school. The players and cheerleaders recognized him in the halls, and for the first time he was invited to a party. On his own he chose to continue to manage the football team, and now as a junior he plans to manage the soccer team as well.

Greg is still socially immature, but he has friends at school. He is considering attending school social events, but he makes no promises. He recently went on a three-day field trip with his classmates and had an "awesome" time. He is active at church, was a volunteer in the summer at a local hospital, and has a part-time job. At seventeen he has finally caught up with his peers physically. He is still shy, and tends to hang around at the edges of activities, but at least he is there, and he has a good time.

Back in middle school, I was a social disaster. Barely anybody was a true friend, and for the most part I felt alone. I remember when I was at our eighth grade graduation I was worried about what might happen if I sat with my classmates. I tried to sit only with a friend and my family who came to help celebrate our graduation, but they convinced me to sit with the other kids. It wasn't such a bad idea. They really didn't bother me at all. The graduation party was great.

When I was entering high school, I was worried about the new surroundings, but most important of all, the kids. I hoped I could start fresh, and I knew everybody around me was anxious to get to know some people for possible friendships. I was shy at first, but everything seemed to get off to a good start. The kids were pretty nice to me. Of course there were some disagreements, but it wasn't even half as bad as it was at middle school.

But by spring my parents were bugging me to get involved in something after school. I still hadn't found anything. I felt I wasn't good enough for any of the sports, and I wasn't interested in anything else. Dr. Peters convinced me to help our varsity football team. That's when I got pretty popular with my peers. I gained respect from the team and the cheerleaders. I remember times when they would clap for me when I came into the locker room. That made me feel wanted. That was new for me! I also found that going to the football games was extremely fun and entertaining. I felt more connected to my school. My social life got a whole lot better—I got invited to parties for the first time since our move. I still get nervous about going, but it feels good to be invited.

Dale Carnegie's *How to Win Friends and Influence People* was the text for our anti-shy effort, and I role-played many of Carnegie's ideas with Alicia. We discussed using other people's names as often as possible, questioning them about their interests (which to her was much easier to do than talk about her own interests), and trying to make other people feel important. When she had the opportunity to use these skills and chose not to, her parents gave her Bad Points, but also praised her when she did take social risks.

The family came back three weeks after beginning the program. I wish I could say that Alicia had made great strides and was comfortable with peers, but she wasn't. She continued to receive Bad Points for missed social opportunities. Some things had improved—she looked right at me as she spoke! Alicia had joined her church youth group earlier and had been attending meetings regularly. The leader had reported to her parents that she was quiet and appeared uneasy, but over the three weeks she began to become more involved. She even quit complaining about having to go to the group on Sunday evenings.

Alicia will most likely never be student class president or even comfortable in new situations. But because of the behavioral skills she is learning, she will come across to others as more interested (and therefore appear to be more interesting herself) and less anxious. Shyness is a strong genetic trait; many parents can tell if their youngster is shy by three or four months of age. It is one of the core traits that colors one's personality throughout life. But by using behavior management techniques parents can encourage their shy kids to slowly take minimum social risks. And success breeds success. Once the child feels comfortable in one social situation, she is emotionally available to try another. I accept and respect shyness, but I feel it's important to help socially anxious kids learn the tricks of "appearing" less fearful. Many have "faked it until they made it," motivated by a behavioral program.

Shy kids like Alicia and miserable wallowers like Justin can benefit from behavior management systems. Indeed, most children need the structure such a program provides. Rules and consequences are clear, and it's easy for kids to make the decision to remain the same or try a new behavior. There's no guarantee that the appropriate decision will be made, but at least the child has the clear option to choose which way to go and the knowledge of what consequences will occur.

A BEHAVIORAL APPROACH TO
ATTENTION DEFICIT DISORDER

Attention deficit disorder (ADD; also known as attention deficit/hyperactivity disorder, or ADHD) has become the "designer disability" of the 1990s. ADD is characterized by poor attention skills, impulsivity, and in some cases hyperactivity. A very large percentage of parents who come to my office have been referred by school guidance counselors, teachers, and pediatricians in order to help decide whether their child is experiencing true attention deficit disorder or whether the kid's inappropriate actions are based in a controllable behavioral problem. Often I find that if behavior management techniques are employed at home and at school the child's actions improve and it becomes obvious that ADD is not the problem, that the behavior stems from poor habits or lack of self-control. To determine proper treatment it's important to distinguish the noncompliant behavior of the child with ADD from the willful misbehavior of a kid with a conduct problem, such as the wandering-conscience or if-then kid.

Willfully noncompliant children can clearly control their behavior if motivated, whereas the youngster with ADD may not be able to consistently comply, especially in overstimulating or chaotic environments. Sequential instructions such as "make your bed, get ready for school, and pack your lunch" may need to be broken down into smaller components, since the ADD child may forget some of the requested tasks. Punishing the youngster for noncompliance if he has actually forgotten the request is not fair, and that's why I usually begin treatment with the behavior management program in order to determine whether the child's behavior can be controlled if he is motivated to do so.

Parents are easily frustrated by ADD kids since many of these children experience abrupt mood swings in addition to their impulsivity, inattention, and noncompliance. Teachers often do not know how to handle ADD kids, especially those who are hyperactive. Without early identification and proper treatment, the consequences of ADD can be serious: depression, conduct disorder, and most important, school failure. An evaluation is necessary to determine if your child has true ADD or if the disorganization and noncompliance are due to behavioral problems. Your pediatrician is a good place to start in order to get a proper referral for evaluation.

Depending upon the source, the statistics for the number of school-age children with attention deficit disorder range from 3 to 5 percent (Ch.A.D.D.) to 10 to 12 (United Nations Commission) percent of boys aged six to fourteen. Medications are often used for the treatment of ADD, the most common being Ritalin, a psychostimulant. The use of methylphenidate (Ritalin and its generic versions) has increased 60 percent from 1993 to 1995, leading the United Nations commission to warn that this drug may be overprescribed, especially in the United States.

Previously, pediatricians and child care workers felt that ADD disappeared at puberty. We now know that many of the symptoms continue well into adulthood for 30 to 70 percent of people diagnosed. These adults may still experience some of the same difficulties they did as children.

In the past attention deficit disorder was portrayed as a subtype of learning disability. Educators now feel that this is not accurate.

Children with ADD are often just not *available* for learning. However, many kids who have ADD need attention for learning disabilities as well.

If not diagnosed and treated, children with ADD may develop significant emotional difficulties as they are often misunderstood and may feel like failures. The self-esteem of children with ADD is at risk since they tend to feel criticized and unable to perform well in school.

The causes of attention deficit disorder are still unclear, but most researchers feel that ADD is due to a neurobiological disorder and not caused by the home or school environments. The *New England Journal of Medicine* published the results of a National Institute for Mental Health study which used advanced brain imaging techniques (PET scans) to compare the brain metabolism of adults with ADD and those without ADD. It was documented that adults with ADD utilized glucose (the brain's energy source) at a lesser rate than did adults without ADD. The researchers suggested that this reduced brain metabolism rate was greatest in the area of the brain specializing in attention, motor control, and inhibition of responses.

Attention Deficit Disorder

Sam's Mom

My thirteen-year-old son Sam has attention deficit disorder, and his ability to behave has never been what you call a sure thing. Although somewhere in his brain he is aware of the consequences of his actions, he is not always able to access that knowledge in time to thwart unacceptable behavior. Our goal has been to make him motivated by his conscience rather than by the attention that comes from the disruption he creates. We do this by using Dr. Peters's behavior management chart. The proper medications have helped Sam tremendously, but they alone are not enough.

The chart provides Sam with a clear list of rules and duties, plus a Daily Reward or loss of privileges depending on how he fulfills his responsibilities. There is also a list of behaviors that are considered "biggie" infractions—lying, stealing. The punishment for these is immediate and, for Sam, pretty hard to take. We have agreed that when a biggie rule is broken, Sam will automatically lose a CD. This means that we throw it away the same day in a public garbage can away from our home. This has really had an impact on bringing Sam's impulsivity under control.

The chart has also prevented a lot of arguments. When Sam does misbehave, we are able to discuss what happened and put things into perspective, because the punishment has been agreed upon previously. We understand that tomorrow is a fresh start, and that neither the misbehavior nor the punishment is personally directed at anyone. Since the rewards and punishments are stable, consistent, and repetitive, Sam's responsibilities have become second nature to him. His ability to think before he acts has improved one hundred times over. Sam has become much more open and honest about what is happening when he misbehaves, and we are able to come up with new ideas to help him when we know he will encounter a similar situation again.

I used to feel very angry, embarrassed, and humiliated when Sam would misbehave at school. Sam's teachers would see how outraged I was at Sam's apparent lack of respect for them and the classroom, and they felt that I was responding properly. But by responding the way I did, I was still providing Sam with the attention he was seeking. When you are frustrated and angered daily by your child, it becomes the focal point of the relationship. By the time you calm down and get through all the things he has done wrong that day, there is no time or emotion left for what he did right.

We have found that the chart helps to lessen the explosion. If a mistake is made, the consequences are clear, concise, and immediate. There is no need to yell or blow up with frustration. The situation is handled for you and your child, and you can both start fresh the next day. I know that Sam had to have some support to help his self-esteem bounce back. When I was as angry with him as his teachers were, I *wasn't able to say to him, "I am sorry that you had a rough day, but I know that you will do your best tomorrow." Sam needed me to tell him that I don't expect him to be perfect, just to try his best, and that I love him anyway. I can do that now, since he's learning to control his impulsive behavior.*

Sam

Ever since I have started on the chart I have improved a lot. I hated the chart at first because I never had any chores before, but now I'm really used to it. I didn't like Saturday as my big chore day because of cartoons and everything, but now I can get my chores done much quicker. Another thing that really helped me was the homework calendar. Every day you just write your assignments down and then have the teacher sign it.

It's really weird because sometimes I can stop and think about what I am doing. But then there are other times when I just can't stop and think to save my life. It almost seems like I drift in and out, and occasionally something comes along and I am nowhere to be found. I'm working hard on controlling my behavior. It feels good when I am able to, and my parents really appreciate it.

According to the fourth edition of the *Diagnostic and Statistical Manual of Mental Disorders,*[1] attention deficit disorder is divided into three subtypes:

1. Hyperactive-impulsive.

2. Inattentive.

3. Combined (meeting the criteria
   for both of the above types).

The criteria for diagnosis for either type are six or more of the following symptoms having persisted for at least six months to a

---

[1] *American Psychiatric Association,* Diagnostic and Statistical Manual of Mental Disorders, *4th ed. (Washington, D.C.: American Psychiatric Association, 1994), 80.*

degree that is inconsistent with the child's developmental level. And the symptoms must have begun before age seven and occur in two or more settings, such as school and home.

Attention Deficit Disorder—Hyperactive-Impulsive Type[2]

Hyperactive:

1. Often fidgets with hands or feet or squirms in seat.
2. Often leaves seat in classroom or in other situations in which remaining seated is expected.
3. Often runs about or climbs excessively in situations in which it is inappropriate (in adolescents or adults, may be limited to subjective feelings of restlessness).
4. Often has difficulty playing or engaging in leisure activities quietly.
5. Is often on the go or often acts as if driven by a motor.
6. Often talks excessively.

Impulsive:

1. Often blurts out answers before questions are completed.
2. Often has difficulty awaiting turn.
3. Often interrupts or intrudes on others (for example, butts into conversations or games).

It is easier to diagnose the youngster with the hyperactive-impulsive type of ADD than the inattentive type. Hyperactive kids squirm and fidget, tend to talk excessively, and move about without apparent forethought. Preschoolers with impulsive hyper-

---

[2]American Psychiatric Association, Diagnostic and Statistical Manual of Mental Disorders, 4th ed. (Washington, D.C.: American Psychiatric Association, 1994), 80.

activity are intense in these behaviors, but school-age children seem to tone it down, although it is still difficult for them to remain seated and to stop squirming. They fidget with almost anything that is in reach of their hands, and have a tendency to touch others. The impulsivity is seen as impatience, with the kids interrupting and often blurting out answers before they have been called upon. They tend to have more accidents than other children, such as walking into walls, touching a hot iron, or engaging in potentially dangerous activities without thinking about what could happen.

Ryan

Ryan had always seemed to be an extremely active youngster to his parents, Don and Rosie. It was difficult for him to stay still even as a baby. Don and Rosie noted that he seemed to walk without having crawled first, and got into everything—their normal child-proofing measures were not effective. Ryan could scale a bookshelf in the blink of an eye. He was often found on top of the washing machine, reaching detergents on the shelf above. Twice the paramedics had to be called when Ryan ingested toxic chemicals. He had to have his stomach pumped, and even though this medical treatment had been uncomfortable, Ryan did not seem to learn from his experience. His parents finally had to remove all cleaning agents, locking them in a cabinet.

Don and Rosie installed locks on every door so that Ryan could not leave the home without their knowledge. Previously they had found the door open and Ryan gone. Conscientious neighbors would bring him home, or Don and Rosie would find him riding his tricycle near the street. They became concerned for his safety and contacted their pediatrician. The physician said that Ryan was indeed very curious and active for his age, but felt that at four years old it was too early to diagnose attention deficit disorder—hyperactive type. The pediatrician agreed that greater than ordinary supervision would be necessary until Ryan "outgrew his excessive activity and impulsivity level." Perhaps later he could be diagnosed as having ADD and medical treatment could be initiated.

When Ryan entered preschool at age four, his behavior continued to be uncontrollable. Rosie and Don brought him to my office at that time since the teacher had felt that he was not learning properly. I began a behavior management program with the family, a simple system that I use for very young children. Ryan performed a little better on this program, but still did not learn from experience and continued to be hyperactive and impulsive.

I followed Ryan in therapy as he went through kindergarten and first grade. By this time he was doing poorly in academic fundamentals such as phonics and mathematic foundations. Although Ryan's intelligence test showed that his IQ was above average, it was difficult for him to sit still long enough to listen to what the teacher was discussing. In addition, Ryan had difficulty with interrupting because he was so impulsive—he constantly interrupted his father while he was on the phone and he blurted out answers in the classroom. Dinner time was chaotic because Ryan had trouble sitting still and was usually out of his seat getting a drink or going to the bathroom.

When Ryan turned seven I tried the behavior management program, setting up daily expectations for him at home and at school such as doing as told when asked, not talking back, and paying attention to the teacher. The behavior chart helped Ryan to get his chores done on time and to curb some of his impulsive behavior. He didn't like receiving Bad Points, and he worked hard to earn a Good Day. His parents thought that it improved his behavior about 50 percent both at home and at school, where his teacher used a behavioral system also. However, Don and Rosie wanted Ryan to be able to work to his full potential, so we decided to include medication as part of his treatment plan.

Ryan's pediatrician chose to place him on Ritalin, although several other medications are commonly used, such as Dexedrine, Cylert, Clonidine, and various antidepressants. Ritalin tends to have the fewest side effects, and his pediatrician was most familiar with it. Don and Rosie started Ryan on the medication on a Saturday morning and called me that evening. Even though he was not in school and had few restrictions at home, they saw a significant improvement in his ability to pay attention, comply with requests, and sit still. One dose of the medication tended to last only three-and-a-half to four hours, but since he was taking it three times a day his behavior throughout the day had improved significantly. They were excited to see what effect this would have when he went to school on Monday.

Like clockwork, I received a telephone call at 3:30 P.M. on Monday from Rosie, describing a note written by Ryan's teacher. She couldn't believe the changes in his ability to sit still and to pay attention. He still tended to be somewhat impulsive, and was more fidgety than many of the other kids, but the change was still a vast improvement over his prior behavior. I told his family that this was a good sign, but we would have to follow Ryan closely and continue using both the medication and the behavior management. The medication allowed him to stop and think before acting, and the behavior management chart clearly informed him as to what behaviors were appropriate and what weren't, both at school and at home.

I saw Ryan and his parents weekly for the next month, and his improvement continued. It was much easier for him to get his homework done because he was completing some of it in school, and he was better able to sit still and get it done when he returned home. Ryan's peer relationships also improved. On the playground he was not as impulsive, and other kids began to enjoy being with him. Ryan's self-esteem improved as other children initiated activities with him. In one therapy session, he told me that he liked himself better and felt that he was actually smart.

Since Ryan had not been paying enough attention during the first two years of school, he did need academic remediation in phonics and mathematics. His parents arranged for a tutor after school, and within two months he had filled the gaps in his knowledge.

I see Ryan twice a year now. He is eleven years old and still on Ritalin and the behavior management program. Don and Rosie have tried taking him off the medication, and he does pay better attention now than when he was younger, but he still misses many of the teacher's directions and becomes squirmy and fidgety in his seat. They have decided to continue him on medication only in the academic environment, since his behavior at home has improved considerably as he has grown older. He has succeeded on the behavior management program since he's now able to stop and think before acting, and his self-esteem has improved.

Attention Deficit Disorder—Inattentive Type:

The criteria for diagnosis for ADD—inattentive type[3] are six or more of the following symptoms of inattention having persisted for at least six months to a degree that is inconsistent with the child's development level.

1. Often fails to give close attention to details or makes careless mistakes in schoolwork, housework, or other activities.
2. Often has difficulty sustaining attention in tasks or play activities.
3. Often does not seem to listen when spoken to directly.
4. Often does not follow through on instructions and fails to finish schoolwork, chores, or duties (not due

---

[3]American Psychiatric Association, Diagnostic and Statistical Manual of Mental Disorders, 4th ed. (Washington, D.C.: American Psychiatric Association, 1994), 83-84.

to oppositional behavior or failure to understand instructions).

5. Often has difficulty organizing tasks and activities.

6. Often avoids, dislikes, or is reluctant to engage in tasks that require sustained mental effort (such as schoolwork or homework).

7. Often loses things necessary for tasks or activities (for example, toys, school assignments, pencils, books, or tools).

8. Is often easily distracted by extraneous stimuli.

9. Is often forgetful in daily activities.

It is difficult to diagnose the child with the inattentive type of ADD. These children do not manifest the impulsivity and misbehavior that kids like Ryan (the hyperactive-impulsive type) do. The inattention may be seen in academic situations as they tend to make careless errors in schoolwork. Their work is messy at times and they have difficulty sustaining attention in both work and play. Often they do not appear to have heard what is said, and tasks go uncompleted. It is important, though, to determine whether the child does not complete tasks due to not understanding instructions, willful noncompliance, or the true inattention of the ADD child. Because school tasks require such sustained mental effort for these kids, they tend to grow to avoid or dislike these activities.

Elizabeth

Elizabeth's parents, Sarah and Michael, brought her to my office when she was in fifth grade. They were concerned about her difficulty paying attention in the classroom and gave me the following history.

Elizabeth had been a delightful youngster, very compliant and desirous to please. She was pleasant and had many friends. She daydreamed quite a bit during her preschool years, but she could be brought back to task when her name was called. When Elizabeth began kindergarten, her teacher noted that she was easily distractible. The noise from the air-conditioning unit would draw her off task, and sounds made by other children sharpening their pencils would distract her. Elizabeth found it very difficult to regain her place on her worksheet and often just sat there looking as if she did not know what to do.

Elizabeth was beginning to become frustrated in the academic situation. In the middle of her kindergarten year, she began to complain of stomach pains and headaches and tried to get out of going to school. Sarah and Michael had a conference with her kindergarten teacher, who described her behavior as very compliant. Nevertheless, Elizabeth often did not complete her classwork, and she appeared to be somewhat lost in the classroom. The teacher questioned whether there was a problem with her ability.

Testing showed Elizabeth's intellectual ability to be in the gifted range, but she was not gaining academically since she often failed to complete her tasks. Sarah, Michael, the teacher, and Elizabeth were frustrated. However, the situation continued with the parents hoping that Elizabeth would tune in soon and begin to pay attention and enjoy the tasks in school. But the inattentive behavior continued through first, second, third, and fourth grades. Elizabeth was becoming more and more upset with herself, beginning to feel that she was less smart than other kids and embarrassed when she did not complete her classwork and the other children found out.

When she began fifth grade her school had a pediatrician talk to the PTA about attention deficit disorder, a problem that Sarah and Michael thought had to do only with behavior problems in children. They had never felt that Elizabeth could be exhibiting this disorder since she was so well behaved in many areas of her life, but when they described her problems to the pediatrician, she suggested that they bring Elizabeth to see me to be evaluated for ADD—inattentive type.

When I met with the parents, I confirmed that an individual does not have to be hyperactive or impulsive to have ADD, but that inattention is enough to meet criteria for this disorder. I performed a full battery of tests—for cognitive ability, academic achievement, attention, memory, and intelligence. Based upon her history, school performance, and the tests, I felt that Elizabeth was showing many of the symptoms of inattentive ADD and should be started on behavior management, medication, and educational remediation. Sarah and Michael were relieved that the problem their child had been experiencing for so many years had finally been diagnosed and were anxious to begin these programs.

Elizabeth performed very well on the behavioral management system as she was a compliant child and wanted to please. Generally she received her Good Day star and earned her rewards. Her only problems were remembering to complete the tasks, and lists placed on both the refrigerator as well as her bathroom mirror helped her to remember what chores to do and in what order.

Elizabeth's pediatrician placed her on Ritalin, which was quite successful in helping her to pay attention in the school situation. She began to complete her classwork and had much less homework to do each evening. Since Elizabeth was behind in some of her academics, about six months of tutoring was necessary to bring her up to par, but she soon was able to grasp the concepts in the classroom as the teacher taught them and felt much more secure academically.

I followed Elizabeth through middle school and into the tenth grade. She is achieving very well and is often on the honor roll. I believe she feels very good about herself, especially regarding her success in school. It has been a challenge for Elizabeth, and when she is not taking her medication, she does become distractible and inattentive, but she has learned to cope with this and to work successfully at home, school, and at various part-time jobs. Elizabeth and I have also discussed her anger at having ADD, since she feels that it has been a burden in her life, but I try to get her to not dwell upon it. She looks toward the future, and the fun and excitement of attending college.

Attention Deficit Disorder—Inattentive Type

Caitlin

I am an eighteen-year-old senior in high school. I started showing signs of attention deficit disorder when I was in second grade. My mother thought that I was just always tired, and had me go to the school clinic every day to drink some soda with caffeine. My teacher complained that I had trouble reading. I was tutored for a while in reading, even though I had a sixth grade reading level. What my teacher really meant was that I had trouble following directions. My parents finally took me to see Dr. Peters. After extensive teacher conferences and observations, I was diagnosed with attention deficit disorder—inattentive type. All I knew was that I had trouble paying attention, which wasn't a big deal at the time.

ADD began to affect me more when I got to fifth grade, when we were assigned more homework. I began to get very frustrated with school. I would daydream all day and then come home and do homework and study for most of the afternoon and evening. My parents and Dr. Peters decided to put me on Ritalin. I didn't need a behavior management program at home. However, I did have to learn organizational techniques to help me get all my work done each day.

My parents and teachers noticed a difference in me when I was on Ritalin, but I only took it to please them. In tenth grade, I stopped taking it for a while because I got tired of taking so many pills all the time, and not noticing a positive difference in my life. But my grades dropped when I stopped taking Ritalin.

After that experience, I truly realized how much Ritalin helps me.

Of course, there are some side effects. I got very skinny when I first started taking it in fifth grade, because Ritalin causes a loss of appetite. That stopped after a few months. In eleventh grade, when my doctor raised my dosage, I lost weight again. One year later, I still have a poor appetite when I'm taking Ritalin. When I try to force myself to eat, I feel sick.

Despite the side effects, it is worth it for me to take Ritalin. I am in the top 5 percent of my graduating class, and I am taking honors and Advanced Placement classes in my high school. I will major in premed in college next fall and become a pediatrician.

I am very glad that I was diagnosed because otherwise I would have grown up thinking that I was stupid. Also, I wouldn't have been able to use Ritalin to increase my attention span. I still day-dream and get distracted when I'm on Ritalin, but not nearly as much as when I'm off the medication. I plan on taking Ritalin for the rest of my life. But even though I'm an adult now and feel good about myself, I still don't want any of my friends to know that I have this problem. I don't think that they would understand.

Sometimes I get very frustrated with having ADD. I dislike having to study more than other people just to get good grades, but I'm doing the best that I can and I believe that it has made me a stronger person.

I hope that what I'm writing will teach other people that ADD kids are not doomed to a life of failure and that with hard work they can still accomplish anything that they want to. I wish everyone affected by ADD good luck and hope they never give up.

Behavioral Techniques in the School Setting

Teachers need to work very closely with pediatricians, psychologists, and parents of the ADD kid. I believe that a daily reporting system is mandatory in order for the child to realize that his performance and behavior at school are being monitored each day, and that a consequence will follow at home. On page 136 I include a Daily Report Card that I use very successfully for kids with both inattentive as well as hyperactive-impulsive attention deficit disorder. As noted on the report card, there are ten problem areas, the first five tending to be those for kids with the inattentive type of ADD, and the last five for the hyperactive-impulsive kid. Children with combined inattentive and hyperactive-impulsive ADD may have difficulties in all ten areas.

Attention Deficit Disorder

Jonas and Margaret's Mom

I have two children with ADD. When we started seeing Dr. Peters our household was in complete chaos. My children could not be under the same roof without physically and verbally attacking each other. My thirteen-year-old son, Jonas, was failing seventh grade. He was totally out of control at home and at school. His teachers were calling me daily with behavior problems and complaints of his not doing his work. He was already on Dexedrine for ADD, but his psychiatrist kept increasing his dose until he was taking 30 mg. a day with no apparent change in his behavior.

We had been to different psychologists. One tried "talking"— Jonas refused even to go into his office. Another had a "sink or swim" philosophy. He wanted us to allow Jonas to do what he wanted. Jonas took this as permission to bully the entire family. My husband and I finally decided to stop the craziness. Our pediatrician suggested that we call Dr. Peters for an appointment. My husband and I met with her first, and felt that Jonas would respond to her.

The first step was to hire a study buddy. This was a high school girl who came over after school Monday through Thursday to help Jonas with organizing his homework. We also had him use a daily assignment sheet at school. He wrote his assignments down and his teachers signed it. If Jonas completed his assignment sheet, cooperated with his tutor, and completed his homework, he would earn electricity, freedom, and three poker chips. A red poker chip was worth $1.50 in clothing credit, a blue chip was worth $2.00 in cash, and a white chip was for privileges. He "forgot" to fill in his assignment sheet the first day. Losing electricity was enough to help his memory the next day. As he got used to doing his schoolwork we started working on his behavior at home. We used the chart and added three more poker chips to his rewards. He had some bad days, but not many because he hated to lose electricity for his stereo.

Our daughter, Margaret, was doing well in school on Ritalin but had trouble doing her homework. Our pediatrician added a dose of Ritalin after school, and this helped tremendously. Margaret was also placed on the behavior management chart to help her do her chores and to control the fighting with Jonas. Her consequences were tailored to her needs—she earned toy chips instead of clothing chips.

As their behavior improves we decrease the number of Bad Points allowed. They balk at this but usually manage to maintain a Good Day. Jonas is now in eighth grade and doing well. He is doing his work independently and uses his study buddy only for help with literature. Margaret is now in middle school and uses a study buddy to help with the transition and the increase in workload.

Our kids are not perfect, and some days are worse than others. Margaret is going through a rough period right now, but we have adjusted her reward system and increased the length of time-outs. I think we will now be able to keep things from getting out of control.

Grade School Daily Report Card

Student_____ Date_____

Teachers' Signatures_____ _____

X = Problem in This Area

_____ Total **X**'s

Problem Areas	A.M.	P.M.
Completes classwork		
Follows directions		
Gets right down to work		
Pays attention to teacher		
Tries hard to do assignments		
Respects the rights of others (keeps hands to self; doesn't disturb others)		
Follows class and school rules		
Does not talk out of turn; does not make rude noises		
Attitude and behavior is acceptable in special classes (art, music, physical ed., etc.)		
Stays in seat		

Homework, projects, book reports, tests announced:

Teachers' comments:

The teacher is asked to place a new report card on the child's desk each day. The child is told that A.M. refers to the time from the beginning of school to lunch and P.M. is from lunch to the end of the school day. As the teacher walks around the classroom she gives the child an X in the appropriate row on the card when there is a problem. For instance, if a youngster is not paying attention to the teacher before lunch, an X is placed in row four in the A.M. column. If this happens again before lunch, a second X is placed there. If the child talks out of turn three times in the P.M., this is noted by three X's marked in row eight in the P.M. column. There is also room on this chart for the child to write down homework and any projects, book reports, or tests announced, and teacher's comments if necessary.

The family contacts me after a full week of doing this, and we average the number of X's that the child receives each day. Then he is told that the next week he must keep the number of X's to a certain maximum or less in order to receive the Daily Reward. For instance, if he receives about ten X's a day during the first week, he is told that beginning the next school week, he must keep it to nine or less. Then he will receive a reward immediately upon returning from school, such as a special snack. If he has ten or more X's on his daily report card, he will lose his daily reward and receive a negative consequence, such as going to bed early or having no electricity that day. If the system appears to be working, then each week or two we lower the number of X's he's allowed each day from nine to eight and, finally, to four or five if possible.

Many times, I've seen that this system alone works well enough that medication is not necessary because the child knows that his misbehavior or inattention will be marked and that his parents will find out each day and a consequence given. If his misbehavior or inattention is behavioral in nature and therefore not true ADD, this should clear it up if the parents are consistent and the consequences are important to the child. Even if the child has ADD, this system will be of help since it constantly lets the child know what he is doing wrong (e.g., blurting out answers in the classroom) and how close he is coming to either receiving or losing his reward.

It should be noted that children with attention deficit disorder do not display all symptoms at all times. The behaviors typically worsen when the task requires sustained attention or a great deal of mental effort or the child is placed in a situation that is not interesting to him, such as listening to lengthy lectures or working on repetitive tasks. When he is doing something that is fun, involved in a one-on-one situation, or playing on the playground, the impulsivity and hyperactivity may not be seen at all. Working alone he will be more calm, but in group situations it is more difficult for the impulsive youngster to stay on task.

What's Ahead for Kids with ADD

Studies have shown that youngsters do not "outgrow" attentional disorders as previously thought. The prognosis will differ depending upon the severity of the attentional problem. Youngsters with mild attentional problems may learn to compensate, and their difficulties may not be evident in their teenage and adult years. However, individuals with severe attentional problems such as Caitlin's may continue to evidence more difficulty with distractibility than their adult age-mates.

As people mature they tend to become less active, impulsive, and distractible even in severe cases of ADD. However, these difficulties may continue to plague them to some degree throughout their life. Continuation of medication, behavioral, and educational management may be necessary.

The adult may need specific vocational guidelines if the attentional difficulty is persistent and severe, such as selecting a job with a quiet, calm atmosphere. For example, the distractible adult who chooses a career in law enforcement may have great difficulty directing traffic at a busy intersection, but may function very well in a less stimulating office situation. Therefore, practical vocational guidance is especially important for teenagers and adults with severe attentional difficulties.

Beyond the elementary and high school levels, several colleges have recently developed programs for individuals with attention deficit disorder. These programs provide a much more structured environment than regular college curriculums, and offer tutoring as well.

Several studies have addressed what happens to kids with ADD as they grow to adulthood. Adults who were diagnosed as having ADD as youngsters now tend to be more disappointed, pessimistic, and lacking in self-confidence than a control group. As a whole, their social skills also tended to be somewhat impaired. But employers do not seem to be disappointed in adults with ADD as had their prior high school teachers. This may be based in the extreme demands present in the academic situation as compared to the less structured requirements at work.

Gabrielle Weiss and Lily Trokenberg Hechtman's book *Hyperactive Children Grown Up* notes that approximately 33 to 50 percent of youngsters with ADD continued to have some difficulties in adulthood. These individuals displayed more substance abuse and antisocial behavior than did a control group. In addition, the adults continued to have shorter attention spans, lower impulse control, and more mood swings than did their counterparts. However, Weiss and Hechtman did find that children with ADD who were treated with Ritalin were less likely to have problems as adults than were those who were not treated with medication as children.

SINGLE PARENTS AND STEPFAMILIES

As all children tend to profit from structure in the home, so do most parents. In the traditional home (Mom, Dad, and kids) there are two parents making the rules and setting the consequences. But what happens in nontraditional families?

Single parents, either divorced, widowed, or never married, often do not have the support of another adult to bounce ideas off, nor do they have a shoulder to lean on when they give a child an agreed-upon negative consequence. These single parents face the guilt and their kids' big, sad eyes all on their own. Thus many single parents cannot stand up to the pressure of giving negative consequences, and so they warn and threaten their kids but rarely move into action with a consequence. Many divorced singles have told me, though, that it's actually easier to discipline their children now, because the other parent is not there to sabotage their decisions. Either way, the kids of single parents need and deserve a behavior management system, perhaps even more so than do kids from two-parent families. Their lives have been disrupted, but new rules may not, as yet, have been developed to replace the old, outdated ones.

Stepparents often find themselves in an even worse situation. Whose rules do we follow? Mine from my last marriage, or yours from your last family? Also, stepparenting often involves integrating two sets of kids (originally brought up with two different sets of rules) into one household. Truly a recipe for disaster! Therefore, stepparents need to consider a behavior management system as soon as possible, perhaps even before the nuptials are complete, in order to let each member of the future blended family know what his or her rights and responsibilities are.

The next two sections discuss how and why behavior management should be used by single parents and stepparents. Taken together these two types of nontraditional groupings have become even more common in our society than the traditional family, and deserve a discussion of their special needs.

Single Parenting

Most of the over 2.5 million people who divorce each year are parents, meaning that *millions of kids become children of divorce every year.* Scary thought. Almost 50 percent of kids under the age of eighteen will have lived in a single parent home sometime during their growing years. Now *that's* really scary!

Studies show that it is how both parents behave during and after the separation and divorce that is the best indicator of their kids' future behavior and mental health. But many parents coming out of a divorce are not emotionally prepared for the changes occurring with and to their kids. Some folks do a great job, but these are usually parents who had it together before the marital separation. Their kids knew the limits and respected their parents, and the kids felt respected in return. As noted earlier, many intact families never develop that type of healthy respect, and when the family splits they may have to develop it for the first time. But the single parent faces many other challenges and obstacles to stability—new financial worries, possible depression or guilt feelings, a sense of loneliness. Many single parents often have so much to worry about personally that it's almost impossible to focus on the kids' needs, at least initially.

Kids may experience many different feelings as their parents are separating and divorcing—denial, anger, embarrassment, shame, guilt, hopelessness, depression, and self-pity. Most children, while they are genuinely concerned about Mom and Dad, are worried primarily about what is going to happen to them. "Who will buy my food and take me to Little League?" worries the grade schooler, and the fifteen-year-old is angry that she may not receive a car for her sixteenth birthday as her older brother did when their parents were still married. And let's not forget that many children continue to harbor hope that their folks will get back together again in the future. I've seen several kids in my practice who insist that their parents will work it out, even after both have remarried and have children in their new relationships.

However, once the dust settles and a semblance of emotional stability returns to the family, what can a single parent do to keep kids on track? How about becoming the benevolent dictator I discussed in Chapter 4? Single parents need to be fair, yet in control. These folks usually do not have the support of another committed adult to back them up, to take over when they feel like strangling a child, or to listen to their problems and to suggest alternatives. Grandparents are generally quite helpful, but many single parents do not live near their folks, or Grandma and Grandpa are just not available to help out.

Marianne, mother of eight-year-old Stacy and fourteen-year-old Matt, told me that it had been impossible to set up a disciplinary plan when she and her husband, Darren, had lived together. He seemed to sabotage her attempts to ground the kids when they broke rules, which made her feel as if she was forever wearing the black hat in the family. Somehow Darren found a reason to take the kids out when they were restricted, which made her disciplinary attempts appear to be hollow gestures.

She came to see me as the couple were separating, and we quickly set up house rules for her new home. The kids had daily responsibilities such as making their beds, feeding the pets, and doing the dishes, and they were held responsible for their behavior (not talking back too much and holding the fights down to a dull roar). Things quickly improved at Marianne's house, but Darren had few rules, and the kids ran wild during their visits with him.

I convinced Marianne that all she could do was offer the behavior management system to Darren and let him use it if he wished to. If he chose not to, the kids would easily adapt to the two sets of rules (or, rather, the lack of rules at Darren's house). They would behave differently for their mother than for their father, adjusting to the climate in each household.

Marianne was concerned that this would confuse the kids or allow them to be manipulative ("Dad doesn't make us do this— he's nicer than you!"), but the children and I both proved to her that this would not occur. Kids are smart, and once they realize what the rules and consequences are, they usually comply. How Darren wanted his relationship to be with his kids was his concern, not hers. She was only responsible for the way she expected them to behave when they were with her.

A trap that many residential or custodial parents often fall into is taking psychological responsibility for their ex-spouse's relationship with the kids. Not only may your ex not want your help, but he may actually view it as interference. If your ex was uninvolved with the kids while you were married, most likely this lack of involvement will continue in the future, especially if it's now inconvenient to see the children. And if your ex was not good at disciplining the children before the divorce, the same attitude will most likely prevail in the new living situation.

If you set up a behavioral system in your home, it will work even though your ex may be a "Disney World" parent, with weekend visits a free-for-all with few expectations of the kids. The children will respect you and your rules, and whether they respond to your ex is *not your responsibility and not your problem.* You may need to post this statement on your bathroom mirror to remind yourself if guilt feelings begin to creep up on you!

Another problem unique to single parent households is that the ex-spouse rarely becomes an ex-parent. To many single parents it feels like a life sentence having to deal with someone who makes you so uncomfortable that you couldn't live together but you still have to work with regarding the children. On the other hand, some single parents enjoy having the ex-spouse available for the kids, because it gives both parent and child a needed break.

Realistically, though, most divorced folks I know continue their bitterness way beyond the final court hearing, and the animosity may continue to color their lives forever. Many nonresidential or noncustodial parents become inconsistent in seeing their kids, which is painful for the children, disruptive to the residential parent, and tends to lead to poor kid self-esteem and much bitterness on the part of the residential parent.

Kids living with single parents quickly learn how to take advantage of the situation. Most of these kids soon pick up on the guilt that you feel for the disruption of their original home. Their kid sonar also catches your depression, moods, and anger. And, what would any normal kid who has his parent in this position do? Well, let's see:

- Play the poor divorced kid role: "Don't expect much from me. I've been hurt, you know."

- Catch you when you are confused or overloaded and ask for a privilege you normally wouldn't allow. You may give in because it's too tough to deal with at that moment, and you can't send him to the next room to ask his father for a decision.

- Go in for the kill—"If you don't raise my allowance [make my curfew later, get off of my back about my grades], I'm going to live with Mom!"

Smart kid, dumb parent, if you go along with this stuff. Never, never underestimate how perceptive your child is. Often they know what you're feeling even before you've figured it out! Remember, our kids have more energy than we do and maybe even more smarts (although less experience), and they just never seem to give up on what they want.

So, is the benevolent dictatorship starting to sound a little bit better to you? I hope so, because it will save your sanity and that of your children. The best way to start a benevolent dictatorship is to begin a behavior management plan immediately. Single parents need their homes to work like clockwork, because there's only one of you to help organize and make sure that everyone is fed, bathed, does homework, and makes it to ballet on time. Kids who dawdle, have their own agenda, or outright disobey their parents throw a wrench into the system. Everything stops as you cajole, nag, and demand that something get done, and if that child is just poky or directly ornery, the whole family pays.

To stop this, use the consequence system. It's often difficult to stick by because there's only one parent, but on the other hand, there's no other adult there to sabotage your plan. If Grandma or another adult is frequently involved, try to convince her to use the program also so that the kids learn to show respect in different situations.

Unfair as it may seem, I'm asking you, as a single parent, to start a behavior management system that's harder to do because you're alone. But if you don't set up fair rules and have consequences tied to your children's behavior, your house may truly become chaotic. If it already is, let's stop the cycle and get back to the control you deserve as a parent.

Quiz Time

Okay, it's time for a soul-searching checkup! You know that you should make some changes in your personal life and family dynamics if you agree with many of these statements:

1. You feel that your kids are running the show and that they only cooperate when they want something from you.

2. You see two-parent families and are envious of the support they give each other. You feel alone and overwhelmed by all the responsibility you've taken on.

3. You feel guilty for the divorce because of the changes your kids have had to endure. To assuage your guilt, you give in to their demands.

4. You wake up many weekend mornings feeling as if it's just not worth it, stay in your pajamas all day, and let the kids fend for themselves.

5. You need help. There's only one of you and three kids to raise. You're afraid to ask your ex to take the kids more often in order to give you a break. You feel that you should be able to handle it all yourself.

6. You bad-mouth your ex-spouse whenever you see an opening to do so.

7. You find yourself buying in to your daughter's victim mentality and excuse her from responsibilities because she now comes from a broken home.

8. You work full-time at a job all day and full-time keeping house all evening, while your kids do very little to help out. You don't push it because you know they'll hassle you, and you're just not up for it right now.

9. You walk on eggshells around your kids and ex-spouse.

10. You've had it. You realize that you deserve a life!

Now—how about some suggestions for keeping your kids mentally healthy through this change in their lives?

1. Don't bad-mouth the other parent in your kid's presence, and also watch it when you're talking on the telephone. Kids hear that kind of stuff but become selectively deaf when you ask for help with the groceries.

2. When your kids speak angrily about the other parent, just listen and perhaps suggest alternatives that they can try. But don't add on to your child's list of crimes committed by the other parent.

3. Keep your kids out of the middle. If you need information (dates, times, medical data), go directly to the other parent.

4. Do not grill your kid for information about the other parent—it will only lead to frustration and aggravation. An exception is information that may affect your child's safety while at the other home.

5. Encourage your child to cooperate on visits with the nonresidential or noncustodial parent. It may be boring over there, and he may not feel close to his mom or dad, but barring neglect or abuse, the child should honor the visitation.

6. *Move on—get a life.* If you find yourself still obsessing about your "ex" son-of-a-gun, realize that he is still controlling your life. Now how does *that* make *you* feel?

Stepparenting

The number of stepfamilies in America has blossomed since the 1970s. The Stepfamily Foundation quotes the following statistics:

- Approximately 35 percent of American children currently live in a step relationship (child and parent with a partner who is not the child's biological parent).

- It is predicted that 60 percent of children born today will spend part of their life in a single family household and in one or more step relationships.

- More than seventy million Americans are currently involved in step relationships.
- It is predicted that 75 percent of all step relationships will break up. The major cause of these breakups are child- and step-related issues.

Your kid's personality does not change magically when you walk down the aisle for that second or even third time. A reasonable child stays reasonable, and a manipulator continues to play chess (but with people as pawns). So what's different? Why do the majority of remarriages with kids involved end in divorce within five years after the remarriage?

I believe it is mainly due to both spouses' naive expectations of what the new family should be like. My practice is heavily weighted with stepfamilies, and I've found that both spouses hope that the stepfamily will follow the rules of each one's original home, somehow magically blending both sets of rules together. It astonishes me when both parents bring kids into the situation and expect them to deal smoothly not only with a new stepparent, but also with stepsiblings who either visit or live with them. These expectations are not only naive, but are generally wrong and therefore put undue pressure on all family members to behave in ways that they are not ready for.

Over the years I've pondered the question of how such intelligent people can have such naive ideas about stepparenting. I've concluded that most rely on their experiences with the kids while they are dating. Often children are more accepting of Dad's girlfriend than they are when she becomes his new wife—for two main reasons: she hasn't taken their mother's place yet, and most likely as a girlfriend she was not trying to discipline them. However, once there is a wedding, kids' perceptions of the new stepparent often change drastically. Many children have described to me how much fun the wedding was and how nice they felt their stepparent was before living together, but now think quite differently since Dad's handed her some control of the family

If you are in a stepfamily, there are many issues to be dealt with:

- Some previously childless spouses have never had to deal with the idiosyncrasies of kids before.
- Stepkids often reject any disciplinary attempts by a new stepparent, no matter how kind the stepparent is.
- Deciding who disciplines whose children is often chaotic. Rules tend to change depending upon the parent's mood or whose kid did the crime.
- Your child now has to share you with someone other than her natural parent, and even if she does like him, she may feel disloyal to her natural father by admitting that Stepdad's not so bad after all.

Although there are no easy answers to these dilemmas, there are some starting points. First, try to understand where your kid is coming from. A child in a stepfamily has to learn the ropes of at least three different households—the original nuclear family, the single parent home, and now sharing her parent with a person whom she might not even like.

The only way to begin to make sense of this is to keep the lines of communication open. If your daughter can at least feel safe in letting you know how she feels about Stepdad and his visiting or live-in kids, she'll realize that you do care. You may not be able to change many things, but kids need to know that you're trying. The tough part is getting her to understand your position—how being in the middle sometimes makes you feel like baloney in a sandwich, about to be eaten alive by both sides.

The next step is to set up a new family structure for the family, and this is where the key word for stepfamilies comes in: *compromise.* For instance, if Stepdad handled discipline in his original family and you left most of it to your ex-spouse, it's only natural for the two of you to try the same routine with your new family. Sounds reasonable, doesn't it? But it's not. Your children may have accepted discipline from their natural father, but they're probably not going to listen to this man, whom you picked out, who takes away your time from them, and who has basically upset the balance of power in the family. If your child was a bit tyrannical before, you can be sure that he won't appreciate one inch of his turf disturbed! That's why it's so important to compromise and share disciplinary responsibilities.

One young man, Andy, exemplified the stepfamily problem. His stepmother, Beth, was very assertive and domineering; his father, Dick, withdrawn and retiring. It seemed that no matter what Andy did, he couldn't gain attention from Dick. All he got was needling and nagging from Stepmom.

Andy went so far as to tell his parents that he killed birds and that he hallucinated. He had been given almost every psychiatric label in the book—sociopathic, schizophrenic, etc. But the more I spoke with him the more I doubted what he was saying. I didn't think this kid could hurt a fly. Finally I confronted him with my conclusions. "Andy, the more psychotic you look, the more attention you get from your dad, right?" Silence—and then Andy laughed. The jig was up, and his message became clear: "I want Dad's attention, not yours, Stepmom. And I'll act as bizarre as possible to get Dad to acknowledge me."

Andy's father got the message. He realized how much his son needed *his* attention and began to spend more time doing things alone with Andy. Beth admitted to being overbearing and agreed to step back as she saw Dick become more involved with his son—and more willing to discipline. We set up a behavior management program so that Andy knew what was expected of him each day and which behaviors would be tolerated and which wouldn't. Most important, though, Andy now had some control in his life—he had quality time with his father and he earned Weekly Rewards on the system. Typically he would request to go fishing with Dick or to take in a movie with him. More recently, though, he has begun to invite Beth to go along, because their relationship has improved greatly.

As in Andy's case, most stepfamilies profit from a behavioral system because it establishes one set of rules for the household and is usually less confusing than the parents' previous attempts to blend two sets of rules into one.

I'm not saying that your kid will like the idea of going on a charting system and receiving consequences for her behavior—in fact, she'll probably balk at it. But you really have little choice. I can practically guarantee that if your new family does not sit down together and compromise on chores, which behaviors are acceptable and which are not, and what rewards and punishments all of the kids will get, then your home will most likely be chaotic, and your children will perceive it as an unfair situation.

Putting all of the kids (yours, mine, and ours) on such a program is the only way to keep the rules clear and fair. Sure, the kids will gripe, "We didn't have to do this before you married Jim, so why do we have to do it now?" The only respectable answer is something like: "Because I am married to Jim, he is your stepfather, and we are going to follow the house rules. They're not just for you, but for your stepbrothers and your half sister also. It's as fair as I can make it, and that's that!"

Sound a bit harsh? Yes, it is. But it's a lot better than the chaos that will occur if you don't agree on family rules and stick to the consequences. Remember, a majority of stepfamilies divorce, mainly because of disagreements over kid issues.

It's important that Stepdad follow the rules, too, giving out Bad Points fairly for rude behavior and also handing out rewards and privileges if the kids have a Good Day. Sure, you'll hear "He's not my father; he can't use the chart." The solution is to have Stepdad use the chart even more. You'll probably get lots of "I'm going to live with Dad. He doesn't have a chart and I won't have to put up with Jim!" Try not to bite and get suckered into that one. Most likely your child is angry at the moment, and it will pass. If you're foolish enough to bite, well, you'll be blackmailed for a long time as your kid asserts his control over your new family.

Most important, don't allow the kids to engage in "splitting" behavior: if Stepdad says no, get Mom to say yes, possibly by omitting some important information. Then go make some popcorn, grab a chair, and watch the folks go at it. The couple's relationship should remain a priority, and splitting will demoralize you and cause you to question why you complicated your life with a new spouse. You probably remarried for many good reasons—love, security, and a better situation for your kids. Too bad that engagement rings don't come with a crystal ball so that you can weigh the new comforts against the inevitable conflicts.

Some realistic rules for stepparents that I've developed over the years are:

1. Try not to be defensive and judgmental. It doesn't work and saps your emotional energy.

2. To be respected by your stepkids, you need to learn to respect them.

3. Understand that while you are responsible for providing a safe, wholesome environment for your stepchild, the ultimate responsibility for developing her moral character lies with her natural parent.

4. Encourage your stepkid's relationship with the natural parent. Do not say negative things about him or her.

5. Watch that you show no favoritism toward your own kids. (Your stepchild has a built-in "sonar frequency band" to pick up on this and won't miss a thing.)

6. Don't expect your stepkids to love you, even if you love them. True love takes lots of time to develop. Settle for respect right now, and perhaps love will come later.

7. Encourage your new spouse to spend time with his or her kids alone. They may have had their parent all to themselves, and now they have to share with you.

8. Stepparents who try to be both parent and friend can be successful. There's nothing wrong with the kids calling you by your first name, but you are a parent first, and a friend second.

Quiz Time

You know you're in trouble as a parent in a stepfamily if you answer yes to many of these items:

1. You're realizing that the kids who were friendly to you when you were dating their parent have become resentful when you now try to discipline them.

2. You assumed that this new family would immediately and automatically function smoothly since things went so well before you married and began living together.

3. You believe that everyone will grow to love one another (and quickly, too).

4. You feel that what you experienced in your first family is irrelevant now. The old customs will be erased, and you will start all new family traditions immediately.

5. You think that discipline will be a cinch—"I've never been good at it, so I'll let my new wife discipline all of the kids. She seems to do a better job of raising the children, although she's been losing her cool lately, but let's just give it some time. I'm too busy working to discipline anyhow!"

6. You wonder if you've made the wrong decision about remarriage. It seems as though the kids (and maybe you) were happier and lived a simpler life before getting rehitched.

7. You resent your new spouse's uninvolvement with your kids. It seemed different when you were dating, but after the dust settled, it's as if you have two relationships: one with your spouse and one with your children.

8. It seems as if there's rarely any time for just the two of you. Somehow keeping a date together always seems to get sabotaged.

9. You're sick and tired of being in the middle of arguments between your spouse and your kids. You're considering locking all of them in a padded room and letting them duke it out.

10. Your ex is beginning to look better and better to you as time goes by.

If yes was your response to many of these questions, please don't throw in the towel. Stepparenting can be the most challenging of all family setups, and it takes a special kind of patience, persistence, love, and a lot of maturity to survive.

What to do? Convene a family meeting in order to set up a behavior management system. The kids' behavior and attitudes will improve. After ten days, decide what still needs to be changed—and continue to use communication and family meetings to try to tackle new problems as they come up. Remember, though, nothing will help if you allow the kids to "split" you and your spouse. They need to see that you are committed to the marital relationship and are going to work together as a united team, not against the kids but with them. Back each other up, while still listening to the children and trying to be as fair as possible.

BEYOND BEHAVIOR MANAGEMENT

The case histories presented in this book have ranged from kids who just need to smooth out some rough behavioral edges to kids who are challenging brats. Most of these kids tend to respond well to behavioral techniques. Even Brad (the wandering-conscience kid) did well, but he needed the very strict environment and consistent consequences available at a military school.

Several times a year I run into a child who is beyond behavior management—the kid's behavior or attitude problems are so severe, or the family's ability to provide consistent guidelines so limited, that behavioral techniques are not enough. Generally I try the behavioral techniques first, but if I see that we are getting nowhere, I suggest alternatives.

I run into three main problem areas that are severe enough to necessitate other therapeutic approaches in addition to behavior management: true depression, substance abuse, and ungovernable behavior, involving the child's willingness to break the law. Let's take a look at each of these individually.

Depression

In Chapter 7 I discussed the miserable wallower, the kid who is in the habit of acting depressed but really isn't. This type of child readily responds to behavior management techniques because the moody behavior is truly under the child's control, and she can be motivated by consequences to modify it. However, some kids experience a truly debilitating depression that is not amenable to treatment by behavioral techniques alone.

Depression is considered to be the leading mental health problem of adults at this time, and is a major cause of suicide. Adolescents also experience depression; some undergo a temporary reaction to a stressful life situation while others face years of on-again, off-again bouts of the blues.

Adolescent turmoil is normal—kids often experience threats to their self-esteem. Negative comments made by peers about appearance, grades, popularity, and athleticism can break even the most confident of kids. Or throw in the loss of a relationship (be it a good friend, a steady date, or a parent due to divorce or death) and depression begins to brew.

Recognizing Depression

Kyle's Mom and Dad

Our son Kyle's depression took us by surprise. We didn't recognize the difference between getting depressed about negative things that happen and the mental illness called depression. We saw the symptoms—insomnia, inability to get up in the morning, moodiness, spending a lot of time alone when he was at home. But these symptoms were not really new for him. As a young child he had trouble falling asleep, he was never an early riser, and he was always an underachiever at school. We were disappointed but not overly surprised when we discovered him smoking pot one evening in his room. We talked with him about responsibility and expectations, and he talked to us about our overprotection and his lack of freedom. Then one night at the age of fifteen when he couldn't sleep he took our car for a drive and wrecked it. If he was feeling depressed about things in his life before, he sure had a lot more to be depressed about then! Of course we realized that he was depressed, but he had reason to be. Everyone gets depressed from time to time when things aren't going well, but most people can deal with it and get on with their lives. We thought our son would do just that. Some more disappointments and trouble came along, and Kyle started taking antidepressants. They didn't take away the problems he had to face, and he attempted suicide. We still don't know if he really thought he could kill himself or if it was actually a cry for help. That's when we realized that our son was suffering from severe depression and probably had been for a long time.

Kyle

The first signs of depression are feeling tired a lot of the time and often staring off into space without thinking about anything. It is very easy not to see this in yourself and can be easy to dismiss or throw the blame on something else. The unfortunate thing is that these feelings can sneak up on you and control you without your even knowing it, which is what happened to me.

It is hard to say when I started feeling depressed, but once it happened, people around me definitely noticed. For the most part I had total apathy for anything that happened around me. The only time I really felt anything was when I was alone, and I mostly felt sadness then. I often sat alone in my room concentrating on the bad things in my life, and making them seem a lot worse than they really were.

I started taking antidepressants, which helped some, but I still had ups and downs. One time I even tried to kill myself. I don't think I really wanted to die, because I immediately called a friend to help.

I still have bad days, but they are fewer now. School is better, and I have a girlfriend who listens to me and helps me out a lot. I don't know what will happen in the future, but I hope for the best.

In *High Times/Low Times: The Many Faces of Teenage Depression*, John Meeks notes common "traps" specific to adolescents that are capable of causing a bout of depression: (1) the push and pull of independence versus dependence; (2) the fragility of teenage friendships; (3) the fluctuating mood swings that are part and parcel of a teenager's life; and (4) the enormous physical, emotional, and mental changes that sweep through a teenager's mind and body.

Going into a blue funk for a few days to a week is not unusual, especially if it is precipitated by an environmental event such as a loss or significant stress. Even with short depressions, kids can be seen to go through the stages of grief—anger, perhaps acting out, and eventually resigning themselves to the loss and regaining the ability to move forward again.

It's when the teen becomes *stuck* in the process, and shows little movement out of the depression, that parents need to become concerned. At this point the teen has difficulty interpreting situations accurately. She may overreact to the smallest slight or misunderstand a compliment as a tease. It's as if nothing can help, and these kids become what I call "yes . . . but" professionals. No matter what alternatives I offer, the answer is "yes . . . but" with an excuse following.

Sylvia had been depressed for about three months before coming in to see me. She had stopped attending school and would sit home alone while her parents were at work. Her school guidance counselor called her parents in regarding the accumulating absences, and they all agreed that therapy was necessary to get her back in school. I had previously worked with her older brother on a behavioral issue, so her parents felt comfortable bringing Sylvia to my office. According to her parents, Sylvia felt that she really hadn't "dropped out"—she just wasn't going to school. She was having difficulty sleeping and was experiencing loss of appetite and a general malaise and lethargy.

At our first session Sylvia looked depressed. I had met her in my waiting room before, and she had appeared to be a cute, alert fifteen-year-old, but now at age sixteen even her clothing had changed drastically—she was rumpled and disheveled looking. Sylvia looked as if she had just rolled out of bed, and it was obvious that she cared little about others or how they felt about her.

Sylvia described her sad feelings and lethargy, but it was more difficult for her to pinpoint why she felt this way. After playing twenty questions with her, I was able to glean that she had slowly realized that the crowd that she was hanging around with was not appropriate—using drugs, breaking curfew—and she had started extricating herself from them. Rather than feeling better, though, she began to feel lonely, because she had not replaced the old crowd with a new group of friends. The new social rules seemed somehow different and vague, and she felt that she would never fit in. So Sylvia gave up and quit caring—about her appearance, friends, school, and her relationship with her parents.

Sylvia was not suicidal. She just wanted to "check out" for a while and hoped that when she checked back in things would magically be different. I explained to her that that was a cop-out—she was now paying for associating with inappropriate friends in the first place. Wisely she had realized that she had needed to remove herself from that group, but she did not expect the intense jolt to her self-confidence when she began to experience loneliness. I told her that she may have to endure a period of friendlessness while she experimented with new kids and new personalities until she found a place to fit in.

We discussed where she might meet new kids—return to school, get a job at the mall, start working out at a gym. But talking to Sylvia was like talking to the wall. No matter what I suggested she responded with some version of "yes . . . but" and came up with excuse after excuse why she couldn't take some risks and try new things.

It was at this point that I decided Sylvia was too depressed to think clearly. To expect her to see my suggestions as reasonable was unrealistic. She couldn't move beyond the lethargy and feelings of sadness, and only ended up wallowing in them.

Sylvia was not the first kid I've worked with who was unavailable to therapeutic suggestions. When teens become depressed for an extended period of time, they often need a jump start to get them back to a place where they can look at their life and problems more realistically. Only then are they able to make decisions, take actions, perceive accurately, and move out of their depression. At times, I've found that antidepressant medication can be helpful, enabling the chemicals of the brain to come into better balance and smooth out the mood swings. However, medication is not a cure-all and should not be used as the sole method of treatment.

Christine Gets Lost

Christine

I do not look back on my early high school years with fond memories. I look back through tears and see a confused little girl who was very lonely. I suffered from depression throughout most of that changeover from middle school and didn't even know it. Depression slowly took over my life after my parents divorced and I moved away from my home state and away from my father.

I did not realize that I was suffering from anything. I assumed that my thoughts and way of life were just my personality, and there was nothing to be concerned about. Yet I acted like a vegetable, did not care about anything, and had no strong opinions about anything. I was so out of touch with reality that I had virtually flatlined and could not feel a thing.

I was very socially withdrawn at this time. I isolated myself from friends, family, and even my own self. I did not participate in typical high school activities. There were no Friday night parties, no football games, no dances for me. I purposely avoided all the social interactions that I could. I never felt like doing anything. Sometimes I even wished that I lived in a cold, dark cave where I could curl up in a ball. While suffering from depression, I actually felt invisible. I honestly believed that no one would notice if I were no longer around.

Days were short and nights were long. Each day I fought an ongoing battle of getting up the courage just to go to school. I sat in the back of the classrooms so that no one had a chance to involve me in conversation. Lunch was spent doing homework or looking busy in order to further avoid the frightening socializing. I would go home after school and sleep until dinner. Nights were frustrating because I would be tired but unable to sleep.

Depression was physically hard on me. I lost a substantial amount of weight. I had been very active and outgoing as a child, but all of this seemed reversed and lost. I was drained of all physical and mental energy. Thoughts began to race and run together, not making any sense. I was void of all feelings. I had to look at a chart with character faces just to try to express how I was feeling.

I was never able to pinpoint what brought about my depression. Stress is definitely a culprit. I once actually told my counselor that I had no stress, but I quickly learned that I was wrong. I was never able to tell when a really depressive episode was coming, or even when I was in one. I think it is easier for outsiders to see what is going on than it is for the person involved to see it for herself.

After months of unproductive therapy, my psychiatrist suggested that I start taking antidepressants. My counselor said that I had a chemical imbalance—that my "boats were not docking" in my head. Even though the medicine would help me dock my boats, I was very hesitant to have a chemical controlling my thoughts. One day I looked into the mirror and noticed that Christine was no longer there. She was lost and needed to resurface in order for me to truly live. That day I started taking my antidepressants.

I am thankful that I finally realized that depression was paralyzing me and disabling my life and that the antidepressants were available to help me. At first I was upset because I did not want the medicine to get credit for my uplift and new self. Those feelings soon faded, and I just wanted to be happy in any way possible. Most of all, I wanted to live my life again, as Christine used to live it.

Once an antidepressant is successful (sometimes your child may have to try two or even three different types before hitting pay dirt), the kid can begin to make decisions with a clear head. If she does make changes, most likely her world will improve and the reasons for her depression will begin to fade. It's important that therapy become intensive when the antidepressant begins to work. The child needs to be exposed to alternatives and options in order to see that there really is a light at the end of the tunnel.

Sylvia's physician prescribed antidepressants, and her response was positive. We began to see the depressive cloud lift after about ten days. Initially she experienced some mild side effects (dry mouth and sleepiness), but these soon dissipated.

Our therapy sessions then were wonderful. I now had her attention— she was mentally available to listen to me. Sylvia's solution for finding new friends was to return to school, and I arranged for her to go to a new one where she could have a fresh start with friendships. Her parents were sympathetic to her efforts and tolerated her moods without complaint. She experimented with several cliques before settling in with a group of kids who shied away from drugs and were interested in dramatic activities. Sylvia, who readily admitted that her acting skills were limited, found a place in the group by becoming a set manager. She became busy with set design, schoolwork, and going out with her new friends on weekends.

Sylvia stayed on the antidepressant medication for six months. Then, under the guidance of her physician, she began to wean herself off it. I watched closely for evidence of a relapse, but there was none.

I've seen her monthly since then, checking up on her moods as well as her activities, and she continues to do well. Sylvia is aware that she may become depressed again, but we'll cross that bridge when we come to it. Hopefully, we'll even be able to work around it by staying in touch with her emotions and working on problems as they occur, not letting them get bottled up as she had let them do before. I believe she's learned a great deal from this process and has actually become more able to take responsibility for her actions and emotions.

Quiz Time

If you're not sure if your child is experiencing a true depression or just a behavioral mood habit, take a look at these patterns:

1. There have been definite negative changes in your child's behavior, either in sleeping, eating, academic, social, or mood patterns.

2. Your child cries for no apparent reason and refuses to discuss it with you.

3. Your son is exceptionally moody, touchy, or irritable and takes it out on you or other family members.

4. Your daughter has always been the sensitive type, but now she seems constantly overwhelmed by negative emotions. She'll tell you about her feelings but nothing you say seems to help.

5. You're getting "yes . . . butted" when you give your child advice. He doesn't seem to have the energy to make the changes that you are suggesting.

6. Your daughter spends most of her time in her room lying on her bed looking at the ceiling, not talking on the phone, studying, or actively listening to music.

7. A kid at school attempted suicide, and your son seems obsessed with the shock value and attention that the child is receiving. He wasn't himself even before this occurred, and now he seems to have focused intensely upon this incident.

8. Your daughter's boyfriend broke up with her and she is devastated. You expected several weeks of upset, but she's been mourning and staying to herself for over three months.

9. Your child has moved to a new school and can't seem to make friends. He eats alone at lunch or just skips it, and the phone is not ringing for him. He reports feeling lonely and questions whether he'll ever have friends again.

10. Your previously self-confident child seems to have lost her spark. She's unsure of herself socially and is beginning to cave in to peer pressure just to fit in with the crowd. She admits feeling anxious and conflicted and has told you that she feels she is no longer a good person.

> If you agree with many of these statements, there's a good possibility that your child is truly depressed. Seek help immediately from a qualified mental health professional. Depression usually cannot be treated effectively without the aid of a knowledgeable therapist.

Kids and Substance Abuse

The leading causes of death and disability in adolescents and young adults are homicide, suicide, and car accidents. Alcohol and other substances are a major contributor to over half of these incidents. Alcohol abuse has been linked to fighting, career and school problems, and legal difficulties. Almost 46 percent of ninth graders report having taken their first drink of alcohol before age thirteen, and over 23 percent of twelfth graders report drinking alcohol while driving. Other drug usage is related to delinquency, school failure, and transmission of sexually transmitted diseases (including HIV). About 30 percent of high schoolers report having used marijuana before age thirteen.

Inhalants seem to be the drug of choice for most middle schoolers and children in elementary schools. Inhalants are found in hundreds of common household products and are cheap and easy to conceal. Products such as airplane glue, aerosol paint, and cleaning agents are often "huffed," and they are potentially lethal.

Be on the lookout for inhalant usage. Is your kid huffing? Here are some red flags:

- Spots or sores around the mouth.
- Sudden loss of appetite or nausea.
- Paint on clothing.
- Chemical breath odor.
- Acting intoxicated or euphoric without evidence or odor of alcohol.

By the time our kids enter the twelfth grade, many have experimented with or consistently use alcohol or drugs. The drug of choice varies with availability and the tendencies of your child's social group. Some students focus on alcohol exclusively while others mix marijuana, pills, and hard liquor or beer. When I speak to these kids, I find that many are aware of the statistics regarding addiction and health and legal risks, but most don't care about the consequences of substance abuse. Intellectually, they can report why they shouldn't use drugs, but emotionally they are not willing to give up the habit. The motto of many of my young clients seems to be "If it feels good, do it," and they're just not worried about the effects these substances will have on their later lives. At age seventeen many don't care about what their health will be like at age forty, and several kids have told me that it really doesn't matter to them if they even live or die. These are not necessarily suicidal children. They just don't worry about tomorrow, and they feel that they have no compelling reason to live. On the other hand, some kids feel invincible, as if nothing will happen to them, regardless of what they do to their bodies.

These three factors (invincibility, not caring whether they live or die, and not being concerned about health matters years in the future) add up to a group of children who don't see a problem with using substances, and they just can't understand what all the fuss is about. Therefore, when parents try to interfere with their kids' substance use, it's generally a losing battle. To compound the situation, these kids can be sneaky, have easy access to substances, and know how to use them without their parents' knowledge. Some folks suspect their child may be stoned, but feel they can't prove it. So until the kid is caught red-handed, nothing is usually done.

Many families witness their child's transformation from a stable personality to the moody, often withdrawn child who is addicted to drugs or alcohol. Most of these kids swear they can stop using if they want to, but truly do not realize how difficult it is to do so. Peer pressure, using drugs for socialization, escape from reality pressures, and pure addiction interfere even when a child tries to break the cycle of abuse. To wait until a kid stops using on his own is often to wait interminably, because most will not.

Parents must take a stand and do something to prevent their children from continued usage. Drug rehabilitation programs are often quite successful. Once a child experiences the stable moods they have when off alcohol or drugs, it's often reward enough to continue abstinence. However, until he has been clean for several months, the lure of alcohol or marijuana will hang over him like a cloud. Old habits are difficult to break, and the habit of substance use often becomes comfortable, as does hanging around with friends who also abuse. Once established in a crowd of drug users, the child feels comfortable, knows his place, and at least feels included in a group. Often these are kids who feel insecure with others and fear that nondruggies will not accept him. It's better to belong somewhere than nowhere, and being with the druggie group at least feels better than being alone.

Kids report that drugs allow them to lose inhibitions—a sense of humor may emerge, or a feeling of comfort comes out. It's hard to break a habit that feels good, allows your kid to feel that he belongs, and in many adolescent circles lets him feel that he fits in. To become clean or straight is threatening. This would necessitate moving to a new group of friends, having to make it through the day with real feelings instead of artificially produced moods, and facing who he really is.

If you suspect that your child is using, then she probably is. What should the suspecting parent do? The first step is to let your child know that you want to hear about the kinds of substances used and the frequency of usage. Many kids that I talk to (when they do 'fess up) grossly underestimate their drug usage. Therefore, I suggest to their folks that they double the amount of drug or alcohol use the kid admits to. If he says he's smoking marijuana twice a week, it's probably around four to five times a week. Kids usually underestimate for one of two reasons: they tend to lose track of the times they drink or smoke, or they don't want you to be alarmed at the actual frequency of usage. You should also ask your kids who their smoking and drinking companions are, and when and how they get the substances, although it's the rare kid who will give you the information. Teens don't like to narc on others, so don't expect ready answers. Concern yourself mainly with your kid and how to help him break his habit.

I firmly believe that an alcoholic cannot drink just socially and that a teen trying to go straight cannot smoke dope periodically. If you want to stop using, you must stop altogether. Kids don't like to hear that. They swear that they can be "controlled users," but time after time the kid slips back into his old pattern and begins to abuse habitually again. There's no compromise to substance abuse. Your child either uses or doesn't, and you need to make that perfectly clear.

If you're not strong enough to set limits on your own child, find someone who is. Most communities have substance abuse programs that are low cost or are funded by the government. Sign your child up and make him go; if he refuses you may have to get help from local authorities. I've worked with many parents who have had to turn their kid into the police for possession of drugs—a very difficult decision for a family to make. Initially your child will be furious, but in the long run, he will thank you. Kids who are using are not thinking straight, and you cannot depend upon their judgment to make the right decisions. You must do it for them. Take a stand, get community help, don't just wring your hands in helplessness.

Kids who know their parents will do nothing about their substance use begin to flaunt it, become cocky, and use even more frequently. Make it very clear that you will not tolerate *any use,* and also make clear what you will do about it. "If you use, you will be restricted. If that doesn't work, then you will not be permitted to see your friends. If you continue to use, you'll be placed in an outpatient drug program, and if that doesn't work, you will be admitted to a residential rehabilitation program."

Once your child knows that you mean business, he's bound to pay attention. It may not stop him, but at least you've been fair and notified him of what will happen next. Then do it! Threatening without following through with the consequence is a hollow gesture, and kids can sniff that out quickly.

If you want to try to curb substance abuse at home, inexpensive drug and alcohol screenings are invaluable. Your physician can recommend urine screens for drugs, and an inexpensive in-home alcohol saliva test is readily available and very effective. Many of my clients are required by their parents to take the alcohol screen every time they come in from partying or being out with their friends. If your child knows that you'll be checking, the odds are that he won't drink. If you get lazy and stop the alcohol screens, you can bet he'll start up again!

Parent involvement is a must. Fear of being caught is a great motivator to cease smoking marijuana or drinking, especially if the consequence is severe, such as losing car privileges or being restricted. It also gives your child a great excuse to use with his friends ("I can't drink tonight because my folks will give me a saliva test as soon as I come home").

Seventeen-year-old Scott was a first-rate student, involved in school clubs, sports, and his church youth group. The all-American kid—except for the fact that he was a closet alcoholic. Scott's father brought him to my office after his second alcohol-related offense—a DUI and a drunken fight. Scott confided in me that he had been drinking heavily for the past year. When I asked how frequently, I was astonished to find that he drank either beer or hard liquor before, during, or after school most days, and got smashed every Friday and Saturday night.

Scott's parents knew he drank liquor, but felt that it was controlled—a few beers with his buddies on the weekend perhaps, but nothing to be concerned about. Shocked to hear of his actual use, Scott's folks couldn't believe how they had missed the red flags— grades declining, less time spent with his family, and severe mood swings.

I sent Scott to Alcoholics Anonymous, to a group that specialized in older teens. It took him several meetings to admit that he was an alcoholic—a term he felt very uncomfortable with, but finally agreed was fitting. The support he received from his sponsor and other AA group members was good for Scott, and he religiously attended the nightly groups. AA works for many, and should be tried as an inexpensive first alternative to an alcohol rehabilitation program.

Sharon, another teen, abused both drugs (marijuana and acid) and alcohol. Her parents had tried everything with Sharon (bribery, counseling, AA, and finally residential treatment) but nothing seemed to work. At the first chance, she chose to use again. What finally worked with Sharon was the in-home saliva screening test. This is a readily available chemically treated stick that the kid puts in her mouth to gather saliva. Within two minutes, the stick's color changes if she has imbibed alcohol of any sort, and she's busted.

Sharon's parents tested her every night for the first three months and she never had a drink. She was also consistently given home urine drug screens for marijuana and acid. Knowing that her parents would immediately find out if she was taking drugs was enough to motivate Sharon to stop using. She feared the consequence—losing her car—and the tests were a great excuse to not use when her friends tempted her.

Sharon is still clean, and her folks continue to test her randomly. She's finally beginning to lose the cravings for addictive substances, but I have no doubt that should the screening tests cease,

Sharon would use again. She'll need many more months or even years of abstinence before the addictive drive significantly subsides. However, Sharon is beginning to think of herself as someone other than a druggie. She's rejoined her softball team, holds a job, and is getting along better with her folks. They have begun to trust her, now that they feel comfortable that she's breaking the abuse habit. Hopefully, she'll respect their trust and continue to work hard to keep it. So far, Sharon's a success—but only because her parents put their foot down and said *no more*.

Substance Abuse

Debbie's Mom

Debbie's wanting to spend less time at home with family and more time with friends seemed normal for a teen just entering high school, but then her attitude turned nasty and she began lying, was secretive, and couldn't be trusted. She no longer wanted to eat meals with us or live at home because the rules were too strict, so she ran away.

What had happened to our peaceful family? What were the negatives influencing our daughter? A search of her room revealed pipes and marijuana. We were angry and hurt. We also became aware that Debbie had been seeing an older boy who had a bad reputation and was very manipulative. I felt guilty; I had always been a stay-at-home mom, volunteering at school and being home each day when she'd arrive home from school. How could this happen without me seeing it? Debbie's behavior over a period of months had become disrespectful and bizarre. Why had she not told us about being in a serious car accident? What made her choose to get into a car with a drunk driver? We were confused.

Everything had become a verbal conflict. She had taken a credit card without permission and also removed the last check in the checkbook to buy pot. It seemed as though each day brought another disappointing discovery. In addition, the police visited our home when Debbie decided she wanted to live at a friend's or foster care. Not only was Debbie out of control, we all were out of control. It felt like water swirling around our heads, unable to breathe, and being pulled uncontrollably into a black hole. We were totally consumed and depressed. Nights were sleepless. It was difficult functioning each day; our thoughts were always on Debbie and the turmoil we were in. This affected our whole family. Even her sister away at college felt the need to leave school and come home. We discouraged it.

Talking to friends and family was helpful. They were extremely supportive and we learned we weren't the only ones going through this unbelievable pain. In addition to the family counseling sessions, we decided and Debbie agreed that she needed to be admitted to a treatment center. We love her too much to think this behavior was a phase or a rite of passage. Some families may be able to look the other way, but it was destroying ours. When I asked Debbie what her feelings were during the crises, she summed it up this way: "I had no feelings."

Debbie

What does it feel like to get high? Is it as good as everyone says it is? These were the questions that went through my mind the first time I saw two friends "packing a bowl." It was the end of seventh grade. I was thirteen years old. As they began smoking, I asked if I could "hit it." They couldn't believe that I would be the kind of person to ask to smoke some pot. I was a cheerleader, on a swim team, played softball, and was going to start running track. They passed it over to me and I did it. I couldn't believe I actually did that! At first I felt guilty, but after a while it was just like another normal day had passed by.

I wasn't into pot much in the eighth grade, a little here and there, but as I entered high school a whole lot changed. I dropped out of all extracurricular activities, my grades were dropping, and I started hanging out with kids that were a bit older than me. I didn't really want to go to school anymore. The only reason I did was to keep my parents happy and to find out what we were going to do that weekend. Who's getting the pot? Where are we telling our parents we're

going? It was like one lie to my parents just kept leading to another.
To tell you the truth, I really didn't care.

To me, I wasn't seeing a change in myself by smoking pot, but my
parents sure did. It's like the more I smoked, the more I lied, and the
meaner I got. I didn't care about anyone or anything except myself.
That's a terrible thing to say, but it's true. I honestly didn't care.

I got so out of hand with my actions that even my parents had no
control over me. I ran away when they wouldn't let me do something
that I wanted to do. I stole a check and wrote it out for eighty dol-
lars in cash to buy about an ounce of pot. I stole a credit card from
Mom to buy what I wanted.

My parents soon realized that I needed serious help. After having
the police to my house twice (I wanted to go to a foster home where I
thought I'd have more freedom), we all decided it was time to admit
me to a drug treatment center. I hated them for actually admitting
me, but as time went on while I was getting treatment, I realized that
it was for the best, and I really did need help.

I'm much better now. Family life is good, I continue with the after-
care program, and I have now been drug free for almost six months.

Many kids who abuse, like Scott and Sharon, do so because of
peer pressure (although they will deny it), and giving them a good
excuse like a drug screening is often a relief to them. The key is
that you consistently and randomly screen for substance usage. If
she refuses to comply with the urine or saliva screen, it most likely means that she's guilty, and you should follow up with the consequences that you agreed upon.

In summary, don't expect your child to stop using just because
it is the right or smart thing to do. She'll stop using only because
she knows you're checking and will restrict her, take the car away,
or follow through with other consequences.

When kids do stop drinking or using drugs, a miraculous thing
often happens. That snarly, moody, irresponsible kid becomes even-
tempered and predictable again. The family relaxes as her grades rise

and daily arguments no longer occur. She may actually eat dinner with the family again and emerge from her room to watch TV with her siblings!

Remind your child that it doesn't take long for a kid to change habits and friends. Once out of the drug culture, it's possible for her to reestablish herself into another group at school. Kids can be very flexible and forgiving, often more so than adults.

Quiz Time

You should suspect substance abuse if you agree with many of the following statements:

1. Your child's personality has changed drastically as of late.
2. She is moody and unpredictable, ranging from highs to lows without provocation.
3. Your son's grades are slipping, his homework is not getting finished, and his general interest in school is waning.
4. Your son is hanging around with kids you don't know and whom he refuses to bring home.
5. Your daughter's circle of friends has changed. Her old friends (whom you trusted) rarely call or come over.
6. Your child is acting secretively—locking her door, refusing to let you see what's in her purse, wallet, or book bag.
7. Your child's personal hygiene habits have changed—less attention to cleanliness, clothing unkempt.
8. Your son dresses in typical druggie garb—lots of black T-shirts with decals of heavy metal or rock groups who flaunt substance abuse.
9. You have noticed paraphernalia in your son's room—pipes, rolling papers, lighters, unnecessary aerosol cans, or even empty liquor bottles. Your liquor cabinet has been tampered with.
10. Your kid overreacts when you question drug or alcohol use. Instead of calmly answering you, he becomes loud and threatening.

If even a few of these apply, get your kid screened for drugs immediately. Don't settle for discussion, get some data. Do it and please don't back down—it could change your child's life if you take control and say *no more*.

Ungovernable Kids

The third main type of severe emotional problem is that of the ungovernable child. These kids generally have a significant wandering conscience. If it wanders just a bit and every so often, behavior management techniques work well if the parents are consistent and the consequences matter to the kid. However, every year I work with ten or fifteen kids whose consciences appear to be so sporadic or even nonexistent that it's frightening to me. Some of these kids have come to me already labeled as asocial, antisocial, or even psychopathic. Basically, they are a crime waiting to happen.

Generally they are not out to hurt anyone, but they have little or no remorse about doing so if you get in their way. They are exceptionally deft at rationalizing their behavior: "The department store makes plenty of money, they're not going to miss this shirt and belt I'm taking." Or "I've heard you were putting me down at the locker today. I'll shove you around just enough to get your attention and, hey, if you get hurt, it's your fault because you should have kept your mouth shut in the first place." In their book *High Risk: Children Without a Conscience,* Dr. Ken Magid and Carole McKelvey write that the asocial behaviors of some kids are based in ineffective bonding between mother and infant, leading to an "unattached child," or, as they put it, a "trust bandit." These kids, not having developed an affectional bond with the parent, do not view the world in the same way that others do. Their motivators, level of conscience, and behavior can be frightening, especially to their own parents.

Beyond Behavior Management

Lilly's Mom

My fifteen-year-old daughter, Lilly, was a fun and happy child until about age six. She had been adopted at the age of one month, and when she was five, we adopted one-month-old Michael. She had up to this time been the sole occupant of a bright and broad limelight. Unfortunately, Michael was a very high-maintenance baby and toddler. The attention Lilly had been receiving dropped dramatically, and she would not forgive him.

Lilly acted out through aggression. As time passed, normal sibling rivalry became increasingly malicious. She hit and punched Michael. She repeatedly scratched him, drawing blood. She came up from behind him and slugged and kicked him.

At age thirteen Lilly became physically aggressive toward me for the first time, and over the next two years she went out of control. She threw needle-nosed pliers, hitting me in the forehead. She hit and kicked me and pulled my hair. She pulled a large kitchen knife on me twice, swinging it but not making contact.

Lilly's fear of discipline had never been great. She felt that if her food and air were taken away, she would still survive—so there! Once after she had spoken to me very nastily, her father went back to her room to talk to her. She spoke nastily to him, too, even though he is large enough to intimidate almost anyone. He slapped her face. She was not going to be intimidated. Instead she swung a closed fist at him.

One day she chose a barbecue skewer as her weapon and during a vigorous physical altercation made two halfhearted downward swings at me at close range. I had made a firm decision never to hit her back, so as always my response was to try to get one or both arms behind her back, get her down on a bed or couch, and hold her still while calmly talking her down from her frenzy. As she grew larger, this became difficult, and on this day she got the best of me physically. After I had taken the skewer away from her and dropped it out of sight, she got me under her on the bed and tried to cut off the air through my windpipe with her forearm. It was, as all the other episodes had been, very scary. Somehow I got her to get up and leave my room. I slipped out the back door and was able to reach my car and drive away.

When my husband got home, I returned to the house. Lilly cried and said that she needed help—could we please find her a new counselor? This would be our fifth counselor since she was eight. At this point we found Dr. Peters.

Dr. Peters asked Lilly to list the four possessions she valued most. Lilly was informed that she would lose one of the possessions for each infraction of the rules. I chose to skip over the first thing on the list and to take away the second, third, and fourth items for two reasons. First, taking away the most treasured item would have been too demoralizing for Lilly and probably would have provoked increased anger and aggression. Second, always knowing that the dearest possession might be taken away the next time acted as a further incentive to Lilly to discipline herself. Within a few weeks, Lilly's aggression had been modified dramatically.

It has now been ten months since we first saw Dr. Peters. Lilly's aggression is now limited to occasional backtalk. Then, I feared for my life. Now, I sleep without fear. Then, we had no civil conversation or shared time. Now, Lilly and I actually ask each other for our opinions, and she likes for me to brush her hair as a way for her to relax.

If taking Lilly's possessions away had not worked so well, we were prepared to send her to a residential treatment center. I'm glad she chose to control herself so that she could continue to live at home. But her knowledge that we would have sent her away probably helped her to make the right choices.

Today we lead pretty normal lives. Lilly has good relationships with us and with her brother. Just ten months ago this was an impossible dream. We have Dr. Peters to thank for being a mediator among all the parties and for teaching Lilly that she can master her own behavior. We are no longer four fearful people living under the same roof. We are a family again, even better than before.

Not all children with severe conscience and behavioral problems suffer from attachment problems. Some, I believe, imitate their parents' irresponsible behaviors, whereas others are born with a selfish, insensitive disposition. I can usually size up a kid with this type of character disorder very quickly—he rationalizes or denies responsibility for his behavior, or has a cocky "I don't care" attitude. As always, I first consider setting the family up on the behavior management program of consequences for inappropriate behavior. If the consequences have enough "teeth" to them, sometimes the program will modify the child's actions, especially if I include a field trip to the juvenile detention center or a day spent observing what goes on in a juvenile courtroom.

If this doesn't work or if the parents are emotionally unable to adequately use a behavioral system to give out meaningful consequences, I then suggest exploring a more intense level of treatment. Many communities offer day treatment programs through the local school system. Often, kids who are breaking the law are also acting out in school, and the administrators are aware of special programs.

Partial hospitalization programs provided by local psychiatric or residential treatment centers may also be available in your community. These programs offer school as well as group, individual, and family sessions in intensive ten- to twelve-hour blocks, five days a week for several weeks or a few months—as long as is deemed necessary for the child.

If a day treatment program doesn't work or I feel that a particular child needs to be removed from the home situation, then a residential placement becomes necessary. I average about ten such placements a year, compared to seeing several hundred kids who are able to modify their behavior at home with behavior management programs. However, some kids are so out of control that the family cannot, or will not, provide the structure and consequences that the child needs.

There are several types of residential treatment centers available for these children, and they often accept kids as young as nine years of age. Psychiatric hospitals provide a safe, short-term (generally two to four weeks) environment where the child cannot leave if irritated and must learn to deal with his problems on the unit. There are family sessions that focus on what behaviors will be acceptable upon leaving the hospital and discussions about the roots of the kid's acting-out problem. Long-term residential facilities offer programs for kids who have tried a shorter stay at a psychiatric hospital, but whose behavior remains inappropriate and therefore they cannot return to the home situation.

I'm especially fond of a type of residential setting known as a wilderness program. There are many providers of wilderness treatment, but the Eckerd Family Youth Alternatives program is one of the largest and most well known. Occasionally I visit an Eckerd Camp and am amazed at the progress kids make. Some of them have been runaways, frequent guests at their local juvenile detention centers, substance abusers, or just plain awful brats who have majored in driving their parents nuts.

The wilderness setting usually groups eight to twelve kids with a counselor, seven days a week, often for several months' duration. The kids are responsible for planning some of their meals, building their tents, and even building and maintaining the commode.

We're talking getting back to basics here. The masks that these kids have previously used to hide behind—music, alternative clothing, bizarre hair styles, and drugs—are no longer available. The fourteen-year-old who thought she was twenty-two can now be a kid again—camping in the woods, taking challenging trips down the Mississippi River, and having to learn to get along with peers and a counselor who is an authority figure.

Sure, there are flare-ups, and kids get in each other's faces, but the consequence is a "huddle up." The group sits on a circle of logs and discusses the problem until it is resolved—a new concept to many of these children. No hitting, swearing, or avoiding the discussion. If someone is obstinate and refuses to talk, the session just might run over, and there will be less time to cook lunch or catch dinner at the cafeteria.

The structure and consequences provided by a wilderness program can be just what the doctor ordered. While the kids learn responsibility for their behavior, their folks attend family meetings and learn the parenting skills necessary to succeed when their children return home for visits or graduate from the program. Wilderness programs are a neat idea, and I've generally seen good results with the kids I've sent to them.

Hilary is typical of the type of teenager who ended up needing a residential treatment center. She is a big girl, towering over her mother, Judy, and as large as her father, Joel. By the time she was fifteen Hilary was beginning to raise her hand to her parents when they annoyed her or tried to discipline her. Hilary had even slapped Judy a few times. When Judy hit back once, Hilary became even more outraged and threw a glass at her, cutting her on the cheek. After going to the emergency room for stitches, the parents decided that enough was enough. They came to my office for therapy the very next day.

Apparently Hilary had been a very difficult kid most of her life, more impulsive and aggressive than her younger brother, Brett, and she had a very low frustration tolerance. If she did not get her way immediately as a young child, Hilary tended to tantrum, and now when frustrated she would slam doors or leave the house.

After her boyfriend broke up with her, Hilary really began to take her negative emotions out on her family. Even though her parents had nothing to do with the breakup, Hilary easily became irritated and angry at them. This usually ended in a screaming match, with her slamming the door and leaving home for one or two days. Joel and Judy had given up calling the police to find Hilary because they knew that she was at one of her girlfriends' houses, and there was really no point in dragging her home against her will.

In therapy, Hilary was unwilling to discuss the situation with me. She felt that her parents did not have the right to bring her to counseling, and she was darned if she was going to talk to me. However, when I asked her to list her parents' "crimes," she opened up and told me how unfair they were, that it was their fault when she became angry, and if they didn't give her her way, she didn't care if she ever saw them again. I then talked to Joel and Judy, and they reported that they had begun to lose control of Hilary at about age ten or eleven, when because of her size and foul mouth they became intimidated and didn't know how to discipline her. Typical consequences such as time-out or taking away her weekly allowance seemed to have no effect, because she would just steal money from them and would leave a time-out situation anyway. Basically, Hilary had been running loose for the last four years, and at age fifteen would no longer listen to authority. She went to school sporadically, mostly to make contacts with her friends in order to get marijuana.

After interviewing the family, I set up an appointment to talk with the parents alone. I told them that their past inability to give consequences that had real meaning had set the stage for Hilary's current noncompliance. They admitted to being totally intimidated by their daughter, and said that they could no longer tolerate her behavior. Their younger son had begun to stay in his bedroom or at friends' houses in order to avoid the fighting and arguments. Judy resented the fact that he had to hide because of his older sister's behavior.

I suggested trying a wilderness camp for Hilary, and at first Joel felt that that meant they were giving up on their daughter. I convinced them that this was not giving up on her, but actually giving her a second chance. What pushed them into a final decision was that Hilary was caught shoplifting at the mall the following week, and she was now facing adjudication as a delinquent.

I met with Hilary, her parents, and her court-appointed social worker, and we gave her the choice of going either to the juvenile detention center or to a wilderness camping program. She did not like either idea, but when she took a tour of the juvenile detention center, she quickly became interested in checking out the wilderness program.

The next week Hilary and her parents drove up to the camp and met with the counselor, staff, and the kids in the group that she would be in. Hilary liked the idea of living outdoors and having to spend only a few hours a day in the classroom. She was interested in the camping program, the canoe trips down the rivers, and even the rock-climbing expedition. Hilary reluctantly agreed to attend the camp, and her parents left her there, returning the next day with the things she would need.

I saw Hilary approximately four weeks later on her first visit home. She was unhappy about being in camp—she missed her friends and the freedoms she had when living at home. Joel and Judy told me that she was trying to talk them out of making her return to camp, but they stood up for themselves and, with the camp's help, made her get onto the bus and back to the program.

The next time I saw her was six weeks later, and she had calmed down considerably. Hilary was getting into the daily routine of camp and was actually beginning to work on some of her behaviors. She told me that other girls in her group were "even worse" than she was, and that she was becoming somewhat of a leader.

I followed Hilary over the next four months, and her behavior improved dramatically. At camp she attended school each day and was earning excellent grades, plus credit toward her high school graduation. Her parents were seeing me periodically and attending a family meeting once a week with other parents whose kids were also in the camp program.

Hilary graduated camp after six and one-half months of attendance. When I saw her following her return home, she looked like a different kid. She was much more clean-cut, her clothes were fairly preppy, and her attitude had definitely changed. Hilary was still Hilary in that she had a sarcastic wit, but she seemed to be more in tune with how her behavior affected others. She now saw that others would disrespect her if she was nasty, and that people would tend to listen and take her opinions seriously if she was polite.

Camp really worked for Hilary because she worked very hard at it. Probably the most important factor was that Hilary's parents finally took the risk and put her in a placement that met Hilary's needs for control and structure. In the meantime they had learned how to set curfews, to say no to unreasonable requests, and to give Hilary realistic consequences if she broke the rules. Raising Hilary still wasn't going to be a piece of cake, but it was much easier than before because camp had taught Hilary to take no for an answer, to discuss problems rather than slamming doors, and to appreciate her home—something she had not even considered prior to her camp experience.

There are other alternatives to hospitalization, wilderness camps, and residential treatment centers. Military schools and alternative schools are also possibilities. *Peterson's Guide to Secondary Schools* is an excellent reference to help find such placements.

If you cannot afford these options, check out what is recommended by your community mental health center. Often communities have funding available for local residential programs. The waiting lists may be long, or the child may have to have been adjudicated delinquent by the court system first before becoming eligible for such a program, but it is worth looking into.

Beyond Behavior Management

Trevor's Mom

It's been eight years since Dr. Peters suggested military school for my son, Trevor. At first I thought absolutely not, it's too far away and too expensive. We were an average middle-class family. Trevor was in his early teens, and he and his friends had developed bad attitudes. We were afraid that he wouldn't finish high school. Things got pretty bad.

When Trevor went away to the military academy, I didn't think I could take it—it was like my heart was torn from my body. But the first time we went to visit him it was like night and day. What a terrific transformation! Trevor is now a wonderful, caring person with a kind personality. He graduated right on time at age seventeen. He had to work so hard, and he developed good study skills, direction, and purpose. His graduation was the proudest day of our lives.

Trevor

I found myself slipping in academics, my attitude toward my mother and father was unacceptable, and I was certainly hanging with the wrong crowd. I knew I had to do something or I would really end up on a dead-end street. I considered the idea of military school and went with it.

My first year was very rough—away from loved ones and having to conform to the rules and regulations of being a military school cadet. The structure of time management—having someone on your back every waking moment—finally sank in. For the first time in my life I felt as if I was in control of my future. I found myself structured, disciplined, studious. Military school gave me the guidance and the mental strength to accomplish anything I wanted. I spent three long years in school, and it was the best thing I could have done. Military school changed my life forever.

Quiz Time

Is your kid beyond behavior management? Take a look at these statements:

1. You are afraid of your child, pure and simple.

2. He's cocky, disrespectful, and could care less about your rules and regulations.

3. The school feels the same way, and he's been suspended several times for his disrespectful behavior.

4. Your daughter has had at least two run-ins with the law and is angry about being caught, rather than remorseful for her actions.

5. You've tried behavior management techniques and you can't control the consequences. Your daughter steals money from you and others, takes her sister's clothes or shoplifts, leaves when grounded, and has even taken your car out in the middle of the night to see her friends. Any consequences you try to use are disregarded, and she's running the show.

6. In your heart you know she's using drugs even though she denies it.

7. Your son has skipped several days of school and will most likely fail this semester.

8. You lock your bedroom door at night so he can't come in and take your money or car keys, or possibly even hurt you.

9. You don't want your younger children seeing this type of behavior and believing it's an option for them.

10. You've had enough. For whatever reason, you can't control your kid at home, and he needs the chance to learn self-control in a more secure setting.

If you're nodding in agreement to even four or five of these statements, a residential placement is probably in your family's best interest. Check it out—it may take some work finding an appropriate placement, but it will be well worth it in the end.

THE EFFECTIVE PARENT

Like it or not, parenting is a contact sport. Not necessarily in a physical sense, but it's definitely an exercise in involvement. Some folks have told me that they think they just don't have the aptitude, intelligence, time, energy, or motivation to parent as well as they would like to. I respond that even if those things are true, there's one thing for certain: they just can't afford to parent ineffectively. If you are afraid to take a firm parental role, your life will be miserable, and you will send into the world a child who will have difficulty raising her own kids effectively.

Effective parenting is also much easier than haphazard parenting. In the short run, life may seem easier if you give in to your kids. However, in the not-too-distant future you will pay dearly. Having to put up with a bratty, rude, and inconsiderate kid for several years is an awful experience. Restricting a child for a weekend because she blew it on the behavior management system is no picnic either, but at least it's over in a few days and next week will most likely be better. And it's *fun* raising kids who know their limits—they are generally respectful to you and content with themselves.

The key points to remember in a positive approach to disciplining children are:

1. *Be consistent.* If you set up a rule, follow it.

2. *Quit threatening—use action.* A twenty-minute time-out for little kids or removal of the car keys for a few days for a teenager often gets the kid's attention and promotes correct decision making the next time around.

3. *Put some teeth in the consequences.* If it really doesn't bother your child, the consequence is probably not going to work. Ten minutes of bedroom time-out pales in comparison with thirty minutes of bathroom time-out.

4. *Make the rule-consequence connection very clear and comprehensive.* Remember, gray areas and ambiguity allow kids to argue that they really didn't understand a rule to begin with.

5. *Don't expect your child to be reasonable.* If he or she is, great, take it. But most kids have a hard time seeing things your way. Just because they don't feel that a rule is fair doesn't mean that you can't insist upon it. If it's important to you, then it's important to the family.

6. *Avoid winning the battle and losing the war.* You may need to let some of the small stuff go (length of hair, clothing style, choice of music) and focus on issues that will mold your child's life (school grades, politeness, values and morals).

7. *Don't expect yourself to be reasonable all of the time.* No matter how much you try, there will be days that you are unfair to the kids. Try to ascertain why you are in a bad mood and do something to stop it. If nothing works, explain to your kids what's going on and say that you are trying to get back on an even keel.

8. *Have a game plan for times when you can't use the typical consequence for your child's inappropriate behavior.* Be prepared to leave the mall early, turn the car around if the kids won't stop fighting, or use outside help such as a chat with the school principal if the usual consequences don't seem to be working.

9. *Be prepared to use nontraditional consequences if your regular ones seem to be losing their effectiveness.* Giving away a possession usually gets your child's attention— and changes his behavior. Be creative. If one tactic doesn't work, try a new one. Remember, you are the parent and really do have more power and control over the home situation than your kids do. It may not seem so at times, but that's because they are challenging you to see if you'll dig in your heels and stand firm or if you'll cave in.

10. *Think of your child's happiness and fulfillment as a long-term goal, not a short-term fix.* A child who grows up understanding his place in the grand scheme of this world will naturally know how to fit in and to successfully deal with his employer, spouse, coworkers, and, yes, even his own kids. Most likely, he will be content and happy. A child who is not given the gift of self-discipline will have to learn limit setting the hard way—perhaps through the judicial system.

Loving means being willing to take risks in order to help your children develop standards and behaviors both you and they are proud of. That's the essence of a good self-concept. Without the ability to choose right from wrong, your child's self-concept is in jeopardy. Loving means being willing to set limits that may anger or disappoint your kid today so that he'll develop a high level of morality which will carry him into and through adulthood.

That's good parenting. No one said it was easy, but there's nothing more important. Your child is not yours just for the first eighteen years, he's yours forever. Why not make it a grand trip throughout your lives—one that you'll be able to look back on and say, "I did my best, and even though we often knocked heads and I had to put my foot down, I'm proud of him, and best of all he's proud of himself."

The values and ethics our children bring to adulthood come from two main sources. Much research has shown that a good part of personality is genetic, and personality plays a large role in setting the stage for a child's value system. Easygoing, reasonable kids tend to conform to traditional work ethics and mores, are cooperative, and see the point in being fair and unselfish. Difficult kids, those who find it hard to outgrow the selfishness of the "terrible two's," just don't seem to get it. They view justice as one-sided (defined as "my side only") and have a hard time understanding where their parents are coming from. The values they develop have little to do with what their parents believe in, and these kids often view their folks as chumps or totally out of it.

However, most of your child's value development is learned from her environment. Kids watch, listen, and mimic the ethics of the household in which they grow up. Parents who abuse substances tend to raise kids who do the same. Fathers who curse or discredit the legal system tend to raise kids who are disrespectful and disobedient. Moms who allow others to take advantage of them teach their daughters to be victims.

And most important, parents who are irresponsible themselves are actually teaching their children to follow suit. The quote "Do as I say but not as I do" just doesn't cut it. If you want your kids to smoke, lie, and abuse substances, just put those behaviors into your daily repertoire.

A solid value system is the greatest gift we can give our kids. If your children are young, start right now to teach them to take responsibility for their actions and to live within reasonable boundaries. Don't focus on making them happy; teach them how to take no for an answer instead.

If your child is a teenager, it's not too late to instill good values. It's just tougher. Your son may balk, slam doors, or tell you that you can't make him do anything that he doesn't want to do. That's okay—just listen, keep calm, and make darn sure that he gets no privileges until his behavior improves. Having grown up with few or no consistent consequences leads to little or no frustration tolerance, so of course he'll blow up. But once the tantrum dissipates and he sees that you will not budge, most likely he'll begin to comply with your request, if only to get his privileges back again.

My hope is that your kids develop good, solid values. As parents, we can only do so much. We wish our children to be genetically "wired" for reason, while we teach them through our personal actions and involvement with them that their daily choices can color the rest of their lives. I'm constantly telling my own kids that "what goes around comes around." I hope they're listening, because I firmly believe that good things come to good people—not always immediately, but I feel that if you work hard enough for something it will happen. This philosophy permeates my life, and I hope you'll consider it for you and your kids!

PARENTING RESOURCES

Alcoholics Anonymous World Headquarters
475 Riverside Drive
New York, NY 10115
212-870-3400
Purpose: Fellowship of men and women who meet together to solve their common problem of alcoholism and to help others recover from alcoholism.

American Association of Children's Residential Centers
1021 Prince Street
Alexandria, VA 22314
703-838-7522
Purpose: Offers referral to residential treatment facilities for children and adolescents.

Ch.A.D.D. (Children and Adults with Attention Deficit Disorder)
499 Northwest 70th Avenue
Suite 101
Plantation, FL 33717
954-587-3700
Purpose: Provides resources for parents of children with attention deficit disorder. Offers support groups as well as many education and counseling publications.

Community Mental Health Centers
(Check your local listing)
Purpose: Offers counseling, testing, and family therapy. Will also help with referral to residential and inpatient programs for children and adolescents.

Eckerd Family and Youth Alternatives, Inc.
P. O. Box 7150
Clearwater, FL 34618
800-554-HELP
Purpose: A private, not-for-profit organization providing residential wilderness experiences for children and adolescents who have severe behavior and/or substance abuse problems.

"Just Say No" International
2000 Franklin Street
Suite 400
Oakland, CA 94612
510-451-6666
Purpose: To help parents empower their children and teenagers to lead a healthy and productive drug-free life.

Parents Without Partners

401 N. Michigan Avenue
Chicago, IL 60611-4267
800-637-7974

Purpose: To promote the study of and to alleviate the problems of single parents in relation to the welfare and upbringing of their children and the acceptance into the general social order of single parents and their children.

Single Mothers by Choice

P. O. Box 1642
Gracie Square Station
New York, NY 10028
212-988-0993

Purpose: Provides support for single mothers (does not include mothers who are widowed or divorced) and disseminates information to women who choose to be single parents.

Stepfamily Foundation

333 West End Avenue
New York, NY 10023
212-877-3244

Purpose: To counsel and inform stepfamilies throughout the world and to train professionals. 24-hour information available (212-799-STEP) as well as 24-hour hotline (212-744-6924).

REFERENCES AND SUGGESTED READING

Adler, Allen J., and Christine Archambault. *Divorce Recovery: Healing the Hurt Through Self-Help and Professional Support.* Washington, D.C.: PIA Press, 1990.

Albert, Linda. *Coping with Kids.* New York: Ballantine Books, 1984.

Albert, Linda, and Michael Popkin. *Quality Parenting: How to Transform the Everyday Moments We Spend with Our Children into Special, Meaningful Time.* New York: Ballantine Books, 1987.

American Psychiatric Association. *Diagnostic and Statistical Manual of Mental Disorders.* 4th ed. Washington, D.C.: American Psychiatric Association, 1994.

Ames, Louise Bates, and Carol Chase Haber. *Your Eight-Year-Old.* New York: Dell Publishing, 1989.

Ames, Louise Bates, Frances L. Ilg, and Sidney M. Balson. *Your Ten-to-Fourteen-Year-Old.* New York: Dell Publishing, 1988.

Avraham, Regina. *Substance Abuse: Prevention & Treatment.* New York: Chelsea House Publications, 1988.

Barkley, Russell A. *Attention Deficit Hyperactivity Disorder: A Handbook for Diagnosis and Treatment.* New York: Guilford Press, 1990.

——. *Hyperactive Children: A Handbook for Diagnosis and Treatment.* New York: Guilford Press, 1981.

Belli, Melvin M., Sr., and Mel Krantzler. *Divorcing.* New York: St. Martin's Press, 1988.

Bergman, David B. *Kids on the Brink: Understanding the Teen Suicide Epidemic.* Washington, D.C.: PIA Press, 1990.

Bernstein, Anne C. *Yours, Mine, and Ours: How Families Change When Remarried Parents Have a Child Together.* New York: W. W. Norton & Company, 1990.

Bodenhamer, Gregory. *Back in Control: How to Get Your Children to Behave.* Englewood Cliffs, NJ: Prentice Hall, 1983.

Brazelton, T. Berry. *Touchpoints: Your Child's Emotional and Behavioral Development.* Reading, MA: Addison-Wesley, 1992.

Ch.A.D.D. Education Committee. *Attention Deficit Disorders: A Guide for Teachers.* Plantation, FL: Ch.A.D.D., 1988.

Clark, Lynn. *The Time-out Solution: A Parent's Guide for Handling Everyday Behavior Problems.* Chicago: Contemporary Books, 1989.

Conners, C. Keith, and Karen C. Wells. *Hyperkinetic Children.* Beverly Hills: Sage Publications, 1986.

Dobson, James. *The New Dare to Discipline.* New York: Tyndale House, 1992.

Dodson, Fitzhugh. *How to Discipline with Love: From Crib to College.* New York: New American Library, 1978.

Elkind, David. *The Hurried Child.* Reading, MA: Addison-Wesley, 1982.

——. *Ties That Stress.* Cambridge: Harvard University Press, 1994.

Faber, Adele, and Elaine Mazlish. *Siblings Without Rivalry: How to Help Your Children Live Together So You Can Live Too.* New York: Norton, 1987.

——. *How to Talk so Kids Will Listen and Listen so Kids Will Talk.* New York: Avon Books, 1980.

Fox, Vince. Addiction, *Change and Choice: The New View of Alcoholism.* Tucson, AZ: See Sharp Press, 1993.

Friedman, Ronald J., and Guy T. Doyal. *Attention Deficit Disorder and Hyperactivity.* 2nd ed. Danville, IL: The Interstate Publishing, 1987.

Goleman, Daniel. *Emotional Intelligence.* New York: Bantam Books, 1995.

Gross, David A., and Irl L. Extein. *A Parent's Guide to Common and Uncommon School Problems.* Washington, D.C.: PIA Press, 1989.

Harper, Timothy. *Labeled—but Disabled? Sky* magazine (Sept. 1996): 87–93.

Ingersoll, Barbara. *Your Hyperactive Child: A Parent's Guide to Coping with Attention Deficit Disorder.* New York: Doubleday, 1988.

Kagan, Jerome. *The Nature of the Child.* New York: Basic Books, 1984.

Lavin, Paul. *Parenting the Overactive Child: Alternatives to Drug Therapy.* Lanham, MD: Madison Books, 1989.

Lofas, Jeannette, and Dawn Sova. *Stepparenting.* New York: Kensington Publishing, 1985.

McCoy, Kathleen. *Understanding Your Teenager's Depression: Issues and Insights for Every Parent.* New York: Berkeley, 1994.

Magid, Ken, and Carole A. McKelvey. *High Risk: Children Without a Conscience.* New York: Bantam Books, 1989.

Meeks, John E. *High Times/Low Times: The Many Faces of Teenage Depression.* Washington, D.C.: PIA Press, 1988.

Peck, M. Scott. *The Road Less Traveled: A New Psychology of Love, Traditional Values, and Spiritual Growth.* New York: Touchstone, 1978.

Peterson's Private Secondary Schools. Princeton, NJ: Peterson's Guides, 1997-1998.

Pipher, Mary. *Reviving Ophelia: Saving the Souls of Adolescent Girls.* New York: Ballantine Books, 1994.

Ricci, Isolina. *Mom's House, Dad's House: Making Shared Custody Work.* New York: Collier Books, 1980.

Rimm, Sylvia. *Dr. Sylvia Rimm's Smart Parenting.* New York: Crown Publishing Group, 1996.

Rosemond, John. *Parent Power!: A Common-Sense Approach to Parenting in the '90s and Beyond.* Kansas City: Andrews & McMeel, 1990.

Savage, Karen, and Patricia Adams. *The Good Stepmother: A Survival Guide.* New York: Avon Books, 1988.

Silverman, Marvin, and David Lustig. *Parent Survival Training.* North Hollywood: Wilshire Book Company, 1987.

Weiss, Gabrielle, and Lily Trokenberg Hechtman. *Hyperactive Children Grown Up.* New York: Guilford Press, 1986.

Wender, Paul H. *The Hyperactive Child, Adolescent, and Adult: Attention Deficit Disorder Through the Lifespan.* New York: Oxford University Press, 1987.

Zametkin, A.J., et al. "Cerebral Glucose Metabolism in Adults with Hyperactivity of Childhood Onset." *New England Journal of Medicine,* 323(20) 1990: 1361—66.

Ziglar, Zig. *Raising Positive Kids in a Negative World.* New York: Ballantine Books, 1989.

INDEX

Mazlish, Elaine, 84
Meeks, John, 160
methylphenidate, *see* Ritalin
miserable wallower, 109-12

National Institute for Mental Health, 121
Nature of the Child, The (Kagan), 56
negative self-talk, habit of, 110-11
New Dare to Discipline, The (Dobson), 11
New England Journal of Medicine, 121

parent-child conflicts, 3-4, 11, 14, 58
  child-rearing experts' view of, 10
  dumping emotions on child and, 24-26
  nagging, yelling or threatening in, 4, 5, 9, 19, 20-21, 37, 75, 92
parenting, parenting styles, 1, 6
  abuse vs., 3, 10-11, 35
  ask your mother/father, 51-52
  assessing effectiveness of, 18, 21-22
  being friends or buddies, 19, 21, 22, 24
  benevolent dictator, 55-59, 143, 146
  can't say no, 3, 10-12
  cardinal rules for, 19-22
  consistently inconsistent, 17
  deal-with-things-as-they-come-up, 2-3
  as democracy, 55, 56
  developing plan for, 18-19
  effective, 187-91
  happiness seeker, 22, 27-31, 191
  laissez-faire, 10, 17, 18
  militaristic, 17, 18, 20, 35
  no consequences, 12-13

nonchalance and, 19, 20, 57, 68-69, 74
  passive, 34-35
  wait-'til-your-father-gets-home, 22, 31-36
Parent Power!: A Common-Sense Approach to Parenting in the 90's and Beyond (Rosemond), 55
parents, single, 24, 68, 141
  assessing need for change in, 147
  benevolent dictatorship and, 143, 146
  children's taking advantage of, 145-46
  custodial, 144-45
  as "Disney World" parent, 144
  ex-spouse and, 144-45
  grandparents and, 143, 146
  healthy respect and, 142
Peck, M. Scott, 12
peers: fear of rejection by, 112-13
  substance abuse and, 168, 174, 175
Peterson's Guide to Secondary Schools, 184
phobia, social, 57, 112-17
Pipher, Mary, 10-11
pit-Mom-against-Dad children, 51-54, 153, 155
poker chips, tracking rewards with, 74, 88-89, 97, 106
possessions, taking away of, 33, 38-39, 64, 91, 96-97, 189
privileges, 6, 28, 57, 64, 72
  electricity as, 89, 90, 91
  loss of, 74, 170
  substance abuse and, 170
  weekend, 88-90

About the Author

Dr. Ruth Peters specializes in treating children and adolescents in her private practice in Clearwater, Florida. She teaches parents how to regain control of their difficult children and how to motivate kids to reach their academic potential. She is a consultant to Sylvan Learning Centers and has been featured frequently on *Oprah, Good Morning America, CBS This Morning, Today,* and numerous other talk shows. She has been a contributing editor to *Child* magazine and currently writes a column for the *St. Petersburg Times* called "Middle Ground" that focuses on the problems of parenting adolescents. She is the author of *Who's in Charge?* and an audiotape parenting program, "The Successful Child." Dr. Peters lives in Clearwater, Florida, with her husband and two children.